GW00597353

THE
ICE CONDITIONS
OF CONTRACT
FOR
MINOR WORKS 1988

THE
ICE CONDITIONS
OF CONTRACT
FOR
MINOR WORKS 1988

Edited by

Vincent Powell-Smith

**Legal Studies & Services
(Publishing) Ltd**

Published by: **Legal Studies & Services (Publishing) Ltd**
57/61 Mortimer Street
London W1N 7TD

Copyright: Legal Studies & Services (Publishing) Ltd

ISBN: 1 85271 145 0

Typeset by: JH Graphics Ltd, 51 Milford Road, Reading, Berks

Printed by: Hobbs the Printers Ltd, Second Ave, Millbrook,
Southampton

CONTENTS

LIST OF CONTRIBUTORS

MICHAEL FURMSTON, TD, BCL, MA, LLM — Barrister; Professor of Law, University of Bristol. Editor of *Cheshire Fifoot and Furmston, The Law of Contract*. Author of *Contractor's Guide to the ICE Conditions of Contract*. Co-Author of *A Building Contract Casebook*. Joint Editor of *Construction Law Reports*. Member of the Editorial Board of *Construction Law Journal*.

GEOFFREY HAWKER, TD, BSc (Eng), CEng, FICE, FIEI, FIStructE, MSocIS (France), ACIArb — Barrister; Co-Author of *A Guide to Commercial Arbitration after the 1979 Act, The ICE Arbitration Procedure 1983* and *The ICE Arbitration Practice*.

VINCENT POWELL-SMITH, LLM, DLitt, FCIArb, MBAE — Advocate; Visiting Professor in Construction Law at Universiti Teknologi Malaysia; former Member of the Council of the Chartered Institute of Arbitrators; Minister's Joint Advisory Committee on Health and Safety in the Construction Industry; Legal Correspondent of *Contract Journal* and of *Surveyor*; Arbitrator for UK and International Disputes. Co-Author of *Civil Engineering Claims, An Engineering Contract Dictionary* and author of *The Government Conditions of Contract (GC/Works/1): Edition 3*. Joint Editor of *Construction Law Reports*.

DEREK SIMMONDS, CEng, BSc, FICE, FCIArb, FBIM — Consultant and Arbitrator; Co-Author of *An Engineering Contract Dictionary*.

JOHN UFF, QC, BSc (Eng), PhD, FICE, ACIArb, MConsE — Arbitrator for UK and International Disputes; Visiting Professor and Director of the Centre of Construction Law and Project Management at King's College, University of London; former Member of the Council of the Institution of Civil Engineers; ICE Legal Affairs Committee; Standing Committee on Structural Safety; NEDO Committee on Latent Defects. Author of *Construction Law* and *Commentary on the ICE Conditions;* Co-Author of CIRIA report on *Procurement of Ground Investigation* and *The Institution of Civil Engineers' Arbitration Practice.*

INTRODUCTION

This collection of essays draws together the comments of a number of practitioners on the new ICE Conditions of Contract for Minor Works — a set of contract conditions which differ in their approach and drafting from the well-known 5th Edition of the ICE Conditions of Contract for Works of Civil Engineering. It is based on the papers delivered by the speakers at a major conference on the new form organised by Legal Studies and Services Ltd; the papers have been re-written and expanded for the purposes of this book, which it is hoped that readers will find stimulating and helpful.

The publication of any new standard form of contract is always an important event, and the introduction of the new contract conditions was greeted warmly by the civil engineering industry which must now quickly come to grips with the new form. The conference at which the original papers were delivered proved a fascinating exchange of views and information and the lack of any real guidance on how the Minor Works Form would operate has led to the demand for this book.

It is not intended to be a definitive treatise, but rather is an overview which concentrates on some of the more important aspects of the Conditions. A detailed analysis of what is universally admitted to be one of the better standard form construction contracts requires that more experience of the form in use. Thus, the various essays set out to explain the legal and administrative aspects of the contract in a straightforward way so that the industry can the more readily appreciate the new Conditions.

Engineers and their employers must appreciate that it is important for the correct contract Conditions to be selected having regard to the nature and size of the project, and it has already been reported that the Minor Works Form has been used for works for which it was not intended. Complexity of the work is a major factor in determining what contract should be used. The contract Conditions themselves are a complex of the rights and duties of the parties — the employer and the contractor — and impose many and important duties and functions on the engineer. The essential point for all those concerned is to appreciate just how the contract apportions risks and responsibilities and to adhere to good practice so that the end-result is what may be reasonably expected.

For the avoidance of doubt, it should be emphasised that the editor merely acted as such, and the various individual contributors are all joint authors of this volume.

Vincent Powell-Smith

AN OVERVIEW

Vincent Powell-Smith

INTRODUCTION

The ICE Conditions of Contract for Minor Works were published in January 1988, together with supporting "Guidance Notes". The new form is immeasurably better than anything else which is generally available in the construction and civil engineering industries. It is refreshingly free from legal jargon, cross-references and the confusion of decimal numbering. Its defects are, one suspects, the fault of the drafting committee rather than of the draftsmen. Like all standard forms it is a compromise.

The Conditions incorporate the ICE "Conciliation Procedure 1988", which introduced an alternative form of disputes settlements.

The Guidance Notes contain some useful and practical comments, but should not be taken as holy writ. They suggest that the form is for use only where seven criteria are met:

- The potential risks for both parties are judged to be small.
- The contract period does not exceed six months unless payment is on a cost-plus-fee or daywork basis.
- The Works are simple and straightforward.
- The contractor has no design responsibility for the permanent works, other than possibly design of a specialist nature. This would normally be undertaken by a specialist sub-contractor.

- The contract value does not exceed £100,000.
- The design is complete in all essential respects before tender. This does not, of course, apply where specialist design work is to be undertaken, eg structural steelwork.
- There are no nominated sub-contractors as such.

In fact, contract value is not (or should not be) the deciding factor. The form is suitable for somewhat larger contracts. The decisive factor is complexity of work; if the work is complex the use of the form is precluded. Whether this will prove to be so in practice is to be doubted.

The ambivalent attitude of the industry towards specialist sub-contractors is reflected in paragraphs 6 and 7 of the Guidance Note; the approved sub-contractors there referred to are not nominated sub-contractors as traditionally understood. Several should be listed for the contractor's choice. If only one specialist is the employer's decision, then he should contract direct with that specialist.

The use of sub-contractors is clearly contemplated by the form. Whilst there is an absolute prohibition against sub-letting the whole of the Works, clause 8.2 prohibits the sub-letting of part of the Works without the consent of the engineer, but there is no express contractual sanction for breach of this obligation, thus throwing the employer back on his remedies at common law if a substantial part of the works is sub-let without consent. The law draws a distinction between assigning duties and engaging someone else vicariously to perform them; clause 8.2 envisages vicarious performance of part of the Works with the engineer's consent, and the engineer must act reasonably in giving or withholding his consent. But if the contractor sub-lets part of the works without seeking consent, or after consent has been refused, the position is not absolutely clear.

In *Thomas Feather (Bradford) Ltd* v *Keighley Corporation* (1953) 52 LGR 30, Lord Goddard CJ appeared to hold that sub-letting part of the contract in breach of an express contract term did not amount to a repudiatory breach of contract, but this is not necessarily the case, and it would have been better to make the position plain.

Indeed, a significant feature of the form is that there is no express right in either party to terminate the contract (or determine the contractor's employment under it) for breach of obligation. This should be compared with the position under clause 63 of the ICE Conditions.

Under the Minor Works Conditions the parties are entitled to terminate the contract only in the event of serious (repudiatory) breaches which go to the root of the contract. They have no extra or alternative contractual remedy. This could raise problems for both parties, eg from the contractor's point of view if certificates are not paid or if the engineer fails to certify payment under clause 7.3, or from the employer's viewpoint if the contractor fails to "proceed with the Works with due expedition".

STRUCTURE

The document as issued by the ICE consists of a short form of Agreement together with a schedule in which the documents listed will form part of the contract. These are:

- The Agreement (if any).
- The Contractor's Tender (excluding any general or printed terms contained or referred to therein unless expressly agreed in writing to be incorporated in the contract).
- The Appendix.
- The Drawings and Specification.
- Bill of Quantities, Schedule of Rates, Daywork Schedules (as appropriate).
- Specified letters as listed in the schedule.

There are 12 printed Conditions, one of which (clause 12) is applicable only to work being carried out in Scotland. The contract is then governed by Scots law.

The Appendix is vital, and is a model of its kind. Bold type emphasises that it is "to be prepared before tenders are invited and be included with the documents supplied to prospective tenderers". It makes provision for alternative bases of payment — lump sum, measure and value using a priced bill, schedule of rates, dayworks schedule or cost plus fee, when the cost is to be specifically defined in the contract and will exclude off-site overheads and profit. Two or more bases of payment may be used in one contract. If Bills or a Schedule of Rates are used, the method of measurement is to be set out.

The importance of the Appendix and of completing it fully and correctly is emphasised in the Guidance Note (paragraph 13) which makes eight valuable points about its completion:

- The name of the engineer who is personally responsible for the Works must be stated. Although he has wide powers of delegation, he is not expected to delegate his more important powers to the RE, although there is no contractual prohibition to that effect and clause 2.4 gives the contractor the right to challenge the delegate's instructions.
- If sectional completion is wanted, dates, times and details must be entered in the Appendix.
- Liquidated damages should be a genuine pre-estimate of the likely loss caused by delay, reduced to a daily or weekly rate. "The

limit of liquidated damages should not exceed 10% of the estimated final value". If this recommendation is followed the amount payable is finite.

● The defects correction period should normally be six months and never exceed 12 months.

● Normal retention is 5%. The limit of retention should be between 2.5% and 5% of the estimated final contract value.

● The minimum amount of an interim certificate should be 10% of estimated final contract value rounded up to the nearest £1,000. The minimum supplies only up to the date of practical completion of the whole of the Works.

● Clause 10.1. provides optionally for the employer to require the contractor to insure the Works to "their full value against all loss or damage from whatsoever cause rising" other than the defined "excepted risks". Clause 10.1 insurance should generally be required, and if it is details of the insurance required and any excess which the contractor is expected to carry are to be stated in the contract documents.

● Minimum third party cover of £500,000 for any one accident or unlimited number of accidents should normally be insisted upon.

If the Guidance Notes are followed, there should be no difficulty in completing the documentation. The intention is that the printed conditions should not be amended in any way. If a Dayworks Schedule other than the FCEC Schedule is used it must be clearly identified in the contract documents.

The Guidance Note makes two further points:

● All contracts should normally be let on a fixed price basis because of their short duration. There is no provision for price fluctuations, but the contract can be let on a day-work or cost-plus-fee basis if this is appropriate.

● Since the contract is intended for minor and low risk work, letting and administration procedures should be as simple as possible.

APPROVED SUB-CONTRACTORS AND SUPPLIERS

As already remarked, sub-letting is possible with the engineer's consent and the Specification can list the names of approved subcontractors or suppliers. The Guidance Note advises the engineer that nothing "should prevent the contractor carrying out such work himself . . . or from using other sub-contractors or suppliers of his own choice provided their workmanship or product is satisfactory and equal to that" of those listed as approved.

This is important in light of clause 8.3:
"The contractor shall be responsible for any acts, defaults or neglects

of any sub-contractor, his agents, servants or workmen, in the execution of the Works . . . as if they were the acts, defaults or neglects of the contractor". The engineer's approval does not limit the contractor's liability.

The contractor's liability does not generally extend to design faults because of the provisions of clause 3.7, which contemplates that contractors can be made responsible for some aspects of design. Paragraph 6 of the Guidance Note deals with this and its advice should be followed. "Full details must be given either in the Specification or in the Appendix . . . or on the Drawings indicating precisely the Contractor's responsibility in respect of such work".

This is an important area, and thought will have to be given as to whether any design obligation imposed on the contractor is to use reasonable care and skill only or whether the obligation is to see that the design is fit for its purpose. The engineer's design obligation is to "exercise all reasonable skill, care and diligence" whereas in principle that of a contractor or sub-contractor providing design is one of fitness for purpose: see *Independent Broadcasting Authority v EMI Electronics Ltd* (1980) 14 BLR 1. Fitness for purpose is a greater obligation than the use of reasonable care and skill in design. An increasing number of cases on design liability are reaching the courts: see D Cornes, **Design Liability in the Construction Industry,** 3rd Edition 1989 (Blackwell Professional Books).

INSURANCE PROVISIONS

The insurance and liability provisions are much less complicated than those in clauses 20 − 25 of the ICE Conditions, 5th edition. The "expected risks" are defined in clause 1.5 and follow the requirements and practice of the insurance market. It is important to inform insurers immediately of any possible claim.

Works Insurance

This is optional and if required must be stated in the Appendix. It is to be a joint names policy covering both permanent and temporary Works and constructional plant to their full value against all risks other than the excepted risks. The "full value" of the Works may be increased by variations etc.

The period of cover is from commencement until 14 days after the Certificate of Practical Completion of the whole Works or earlier certificate of completion in respect of part: see clause 3.2. Loss or damage in the Defects Correction Period from any cause arising prior to its commencement, and loss or damage occasioned by the contractor complying with his defects obligations is also covered. The contractor is not liable to insure against repair or reconstruction of any work, etc, not in accordance with the contract requirements.

The contractor's all-risks policy is probably suitable in most cases, although the wording of the policy is important. Any excess will be borne by the contractor.

Damage to Persons and Property

Clause 10.2 — the contractor's indemnity — is against "all losses and claims for injury or damage to any person or property whatsoever" (other than the Works themselves), but liability is proportionately reduced (clause 10.3) where the employer or the engineer or other contractors are contributorily negligent. In essence the contractor must make good to the employer all liabilities which he incurs to third parties due to the contractor's fault. Clause 10.4 lists the exceptions as "unavoidable damage". Third-party cover is recommended to be at least £500,000. In some cases greater cover is required.

Employer's Indemnity

Clause 10.5 is the employer's cross-indemnity to the contractor covering claims arising out of "unavoidable damage", and is subject to a like reduction on account of the contractor's contributory negligence, etc.

Procedural

The insurance is to be placed with an insurer approved by the employer and the Appendix entry must be completed. If required, the contractor must produce the policies and premium receipts.

© Vincent Powell-Smith 1989

The Institution of Civil Engineers Conditions of Contract for Minor Works

Appendix to the Conditions of Contract
(to be prepared before tenders are invited and to be included with the documents supplied to prospective tenderers)

1. Short description of the work to be carried out under the Contract

   . . . .

   . . . .

   . . . .

2. The payment to be made under Article 2 of the Agreement in accordance with Clause 7 will be ascertained on the following basis. (The alternatives not being used are to be deleted. Two or more bases for payment may be used on one Contract.)
   - (a) Lump sum
   - (b) Measure and value using a priced Bill of Quantities
   - (c) Valuation based on a Schedule of Rates (with an indication in the Schedule of the approximate quantities of major items)
   - (d) Valuation based on a Daywork Schedule
   - (e) Cost plus fee (the cost is to be specifically defined in the Contract and will exclude off-site overheads and profit)

3. Where a Bill of Quantities or a Schedule of Rates is provided the method of measurement used is

   . . . .

4. Name of the Engineer
   (Clause 2.1) . . . .

5. Starting date (if known)
   (Clause 4.1) . . . .

6. Period for completion
   (Clause 4.2) . . . .

7. Period for completion of parts of the Works (if applicable) and details of the work to be carried out within each such part
   (Clause 4.2)

Details of work	Period for completion
Part A	. . . .
Part B	. . . .

17

Part C . . . .

8. Liquidated damages
   (Clause 4.6) . . . .

9. Limit of liquidated damages
   (Clause 4.6) . . . .

10. Defects Correction Period
    (Clause 5.1) . . . .

11. Rate of retention
    (Clause 7.3) . . . .

12. Limit of retention
    (Clause 7.3) . . . .

13. Minimum amount of interim certificate
    (Clause 7.3) . . . .

14. Bank whose base lending rate is to be used
    (Clause 7.8) . . . .

15. Insurance of the Works
    (Clause 10.1) Required/Not required

16. Minimum amount of third party insurance (persons and property)
    (Clause 10.6) . . . .

Any one accident/Number of accidents unlimited

© **The Institution of Civil Engineers Conditions of Contract for Minor Works**

THE ROLE OF THE ENGINEER

Michael Furmston

INTRODUCTION

The engineer is in a paradoxical position in relation to the ICE Conditions. He is a central figure in the Conditions, being constantly referred to in them but he is not a party to the contract of which the conditions are part and the doctrine of privity of contract normally ensures that a contract confers neither rights nor duties on a non-party.

As far as contract claims are concerned it is important to note that the employer normally enters into two contracts:

(a) One for the carrying out of the Works with the contractor.
(b) A second for professional services with the engineer either under the ACE conditions or if the engineer is an employee of the employer under the contract of employment.

A further complication is that as far as the ICE Conditions are concerned, the engineer has a dual function. Sometimes he is acting as the agent of the employer; sometimes he is expected to exercise independent professional judgment. (Sometimes perhaps he is expected to do both at once!)

In effect employer, engineer and contractor form a triangle and we need to examine each side of the triangle in turn. But first.

WHO IS THE ENGINEER?

Under clause 2.1 the employer is to notify in writing to the contractor a named individual as engineer. This is a significant difference from ICE 5th Edition where it is believed that a partnership is often appointed as engineer. Presumably it will also not be possible to make an appointment in the form "Chief Engineer Toytown Borough Council".

It should be noted also that changes in engineer must be notified in writing to the contractor. Clause 2.1 only talks of the engineer being unable to continue his duties. Does this mean that the employer cannot dismiss the engineer and appoint another engineer?

The guidance notes state that it is intended that the name of the engineer who will be personally responsible for the Works should be stated. This is not of course legally binding but it would mean that it would be bad practice routinely to appoint by name the senior person in an organisation.

An important practical consequence of the appointment provisions is that the powers and duties of the engineer can only be exercised by the engineer or under the delegation powers in condition 2.2. The only restriction on delegation under clause 2.2 is that prior notice in writing be given to the contractor. This is in marked contrast to ICE 5th Edition where many of the most important powers of the engineer cannot be delegated at all. In practice one would assume that if the person "personally responsible" is appointed, he will not wish to delegate most of the powers.

THE RELATIONSHIP OF ENGINEER AND EMPLOYER

Consulting engineers are normally engaged on ACE Conditions. These Conditions deal mainly with the sort of things the engineer should normally do in relation to different types of engagement and to the basis of payment.

The standard of care laid down — that of reasonable diligence — would in any case be implied and is the standard generally imposed on professional men in the law of tort. There is a strong historic trend to expand the sphere of professional negligence. It can be assumed that salaried engineers are in the same legal position as consulting engineers but in practice they are much less likely to be sued by their employer.

(a) The contractual obligations imposed on a professional person are nowadays merely a part of his overall legal responsibilities.

Engineers, along with other professional persons, must appreciate that their legal obligations consist of a conjunction of overlapping and interrelating contractual, tortious and statutory duties.

(b) The obligation to undertake one's work with reasonable care and skill is imposed by the law both as an implied term in a contract for professional services and as an independent tortious obligation owed to forseeable third parties.

(c) Contractual duties are stringently limited by the doctrine of privity of contract. The contractual arrangements under which construction work is designed and built commonly mean that the person who suffers as a result of defects in the work is denied a contractual claim against the person ultimately responsible for his loss. The rapid evolution of tortious duties under the influence of the seminal decision in *Hedley Byrne & Co Ltd* v *Heller & Partners Ltd* (1964) AC 465 has meant that there now exists a potent tortious remedy capable of filling this gap.

(d) The main advances achieved by the expansion of tortious duties are:

(i) **Gratuitous Advice.** The decision in *Hedley Byrne* which established the possibility of a duty of care being owed in respect of certain examples of negligent statements, in effect opened the door to tortious liability for advice given gratuitously.

(ii) **Liability to Non-clients.** It now follows from the previous rule that a professional man may now owe duties to persons who are not his clients. This does indeed raise the possibility that in certain circumstances a duty may be owed to those who are engaged in dealing with the client, as well as to those who are simply affected by the work. Difficult problems may arise as to the relationship of the varying duties which may arise on a given set of facts.

(iii) **Economic Loss.** The courts nowadays recognise a wider range of losses as being recoverable in a tort claim. The leading decisions of the House of Lords have pursued an erratic circle. At the moment it appears to be a reasonably accurate summary of the position to say that there can be recovery of economic loss under the *Hedley Byrne* doctrine but not under the general law of negligence – the distinguishing feature of *Hedley Byrne* for this purpose being that the plaintiff relied on the defendant.

(iv) **Dual Liability.** There is now authority supporting the proposition that the client of a professional man may choose to bring a claim against his adviser in tort rather than in contract if there are procedural reasons for doing this. On

21

occasion, the rules dealing with limitation of actions may make this a very significant right. *Midland Bank Trust Co Ltd v Hett, Stubbs & Kemp* (1979) Ch 384.

(e) It was for a long time thought that an architect or engineer whilst certifying under the contract was free from liability. It is now clear that this is wrong. Although the engineer must be independent and fair, he also owes the employer a duty to be careful: *Sutcliffe v Thackrah* (1974) AC 727.

THE ENGINEER AS AN AGENT OF THE EMPLOYER

Agency in General

A principle may make a contract through an agent, if he gives him the necessary authority: the effect is normally as if the contract were made with the principal alone (the agent drops out).

The agent may make a contract which is binding on the principal:
  (i) if he has *express authority*; or
  (ii) if the authority can be *implied* as necessary to the authority given him; or
  (iii) if the authority is *apparent* from a representation made by the principal; or
  (iv) if the contract is within the *usual* authority of such an agent and the principal has not announced any limitation of this authority.

The principal may also ratify later an act for which the agent did not have authority.

If the agent represents to the other party that he has your authority when he does not, he will be liable to the other on an *implied warranty of authority*.

The agent may make the contract on the principal's behalf without telling the other party. The principal may then sue and be sued on the contract as *undisclosed principal*, but in this case the agent must have authority in advance. In this case the third party may, if he chooses, sue the agent; and if he is sued by the principal he may use defences valid against the agent.

The Engineer in Particular

There is no doubt that much of the time the engineer is acting as the agent of the employer. For this purpose much of the contract is effectively setting out the authority of the engineer. This has two aspects:
  (i) as between the employer and the engineer it can normally be implied that the engineer has authority to act as the ICE Conditions assume that he will; and

(ii) as between employer and contractor, the contractor is entitled to say that the engineer has *apparent* authority to exercise the powers given to him by the Conditions. This means that the employer will be bound by an exercise of the powers even if he has forbidden it. For example, if the employer instructs the engineer to issue no variation orders, the engineer will still have apparent authority to issue variations and so a variation ordered by him would be binding on the employer. (As to the position if the engineer obeys this order see below.)

The engineer's authority, although wide, is not unlimited. Some matters are expressly reserved to the employer — see the contrast between assignment and subletting in Conditions 8.1 and 8.2. The engineer has no general authority to wheel and deal.

THE ENGINEER AS IMPARTIAL DECISION MAKER

It is clear that one underlying assumption behind the ICE Conditions is that the engineer can and will bring an independent professional judgment to certain questions and decide fairly as between employer and contractor.

A major example is certificates. Condition 7.3 says that the engineer "shall certify" and the employer "shall pay". It is implicit in these arrangements that the employer will not interfere with the certifying process, for example, by telling the engineer not to issue a certificate until some dispute has been resolved.

Hickman & Co v Roberts (1913) AC 229; *Perini Corporation v Commonwealth of Australia* (1969) 12 BLR 82.

It seems probable that this duty not to interfere extends not only to obviously independent functions, like certification, but to arguably managerial functions like variations and extensions of time. The provisions as to extensions of time under clause 4.4 appear to prohibit the not uncommon practice of postponing consideration of extensions until the end of the contract.

On wrongful refusal to order variations see *Holland & Hannen and Cubitts (Northern) Ltd v Welsh Health Technical Services Organisation* (1981) 18 BLR 80.

CLAIMS BY THE CONTRACTOR AGAINST THE ENGINEER

There is no liability in contract because there is no contract. There may, however, be liability in tort although the boundaries of this are not certain.

(a) Can the contractor claim for careless undercertification? In *Sutcliffe* v *Thackrah* (supra) the employer recovered for careless overcertification although in that case the claim was in contract. Some commentators had thought that by parity of reasoning a contractor who suffered from careless undercertification might have a claim but in *Pacific Associates* v *Baxter* (1989) 16 Con LR90 such a claim was rejected.

(b) Careless site survey and design.

(c) Careless instructions during supervision of Works in progress.

Certainly the engineer is liable to individuals who suffer physical injuries or property damage as a result of (b) or (c). As the law presently stands it seems unlikely that the contractor can recover where his loss was purely financial.

© **M P Furmston 1989**

THE CONTRACTOR'S OBLIGATIONS

Geoffrey Hawker

INTRODUCTION

Although the ICE Minor Works Form is based firmly on the principles underlying its "parent" form, the ICE General Conditions of Contract, 5th Edition, it was considered that, for the smaller, quicker, simpler projects for which the Minor Works Form is intended, the full provisions of the 5th Edition were somewhat inappropriate. Again, as the level of risk will normally be moderate, it was felt that a fairly extensive simplification of the 5th Edition procedures was justified without endangering the efficient and economic administration of minor works projects.

On the other hand, while for the most part such projects will indeed be straightforward, low-risk enterprises, a small proportion of short, low-value projects will be nevertheless of great complexity, or there may be substantial uncertainty about the Conditions which may be encountered. In such cases it may well be prudent to use the full 5th Edition so as to retain the advantages which its more sophisticated provisions make available. Again, if the employer is determined to enforce the employment of specified sub-contractors or suppliers, the Minor Works Form should not be used as it contains nothing analogous to the Nominated Sub-Contract provisions in clause 59A, 59B and 59C of the 5th Edition.

That having been said, the respective functions and obligations of the engineer and the contractor under the Minor Works form are largely the same as those under the 5th Edition, and practitioners who are familiar with the latter should find little difficulty in handling the former. There are, of course, some matters of detail where the two forms differ slightly but the general tenor of the two documents is the same. The functions of the engineer are dealt with elsewhere, so this chapter will concentrate on the position of the contractor.

The contractor's obligations under the Minor Works Form may be found in three separate sections of the Conditions, namely section 3 ("General Obligations") in clauses 3.1 to 3.9 inclusive; section 4 ("Starting and Completion") in clauses 4.1 to 4.7 inclusive; and section 5 ("Defects") in clauses 5.1 to 5.5 inclusive. It will be found convenient to consider the relevant provisions under each of these three headings in turn.

GENERAL OBLIGATIONS (SECTION 3)

The first and fundamental obligation laid upon the contractor as set out in clause 3.1 is to perform and complete the Works. Indeed, this must be so, as that is precisely what the employer is paying for and would arise in any event as a necessary implication of law. The analogous clause 8(1) in the 5th Edition is slightly wider in that it requires the contractor to "construct, complete and maintain" the works whereas clause 3.1 only requires him to "perform and complete" them. Nevertheless, the 5th Edition requirement to "maintain" them has not been omitted, as it appears in a slightly different form in Minor Works clause 4.7.

Clause 3.1 further requires the contractor to provide all necessary supervision, labour, materials, plant, transport and temporary works, thereby combining the rest of 5th Edition clause 8(1) with the subtance of clause 15(1). However, as in the 5th Edition, it is possible to relieve the contractor from any of these requirements by inserting a special provision to that effect, either as an additional special clause or by making appropriate provision in the specification.

In addition to the foregoing obligations, clause 3.2 requires the contractor to care for the Works from their commencement (see clause 4.1) until 14 days after they are completed. In this it reflects and is essentially on all fours with clause 20(1) of the 5th Edition. By "completion" is meant the issue by the engineer under clause 4.5 of a Certificate of Practical Completion for the whole of the Works. As in the 5th Edition, the 14 day overrun of the contractor's responsibility is intended to give the employer time to take out such insurance as may be necessary to cover the Works as completed, since the contractor is only bound under the contract to insure the period for which he is responsible.

It is frequently the case that a part or parts of the Works may be physically completed before the whole of the Works are finished, and it may well be convenient for such parts to be handed over to the employer in advance of the final handover. In such cases clause 3.2(2) provides that where appropriate Completion Certificates are forthcoming, the 14 dayhand over procedure will take place before final completion.

Notwithstanding such handovers, the contractor will remain responsible for the care of any work which may be outstanding at the date of practical completion and which he has undertaken to finish during the Defects Correction Period (as the 5th Edition's Maintenance Period is now called) until such outstanding work is complete (clause 3.2(3)). However, such continuing responsibility ceases as soon as the work to which it refers is finished; no 14 day overlap is necessary as the main 14 day overlap under clauses 3.2(1) or 3.2(2) will already have expired and the overall insurance risk will have passed to the employer.

As well as being responsible for the care of the Works, the contractor is by clause 3.3 required to repair and make good "any damage, loss or injury [which] shall happen to the Works or any part thereof" during this period of responsibility. This requirement is the same as that imposed by the 5th Edition. Moreover, the contractor must repair all such damage, loss or injury whatever the cause may be (clause 3.3(1)) so as to ensure that upon completion the Works are in good order and condition, and conform in every respect with both the requirements of the contract and the engineer's instructions. However, to the extent that a part or parts of the Works may have been completed early and have been taken over by the employer, the contractor will not be responsible for rectifying anything which is the direct and usual result of the employer's use and/or occupation or, to put it another way, clause 3.3 does not require the contractor to counter the effects of fair wear and tear after handover to the employer.

Such repairs are all to be carried out at the contractor's own cost (clause 3.3(1)), as are repairs resulting from damage arising after handover (clause 3.3(3)) occasioned by his performance of obligations under clauses 4.7 (rectification of defects) and 5.2 (defects due to substandard materials or workmanship). This will be so unless the contractor can show that the damage, loss or injury arose from any of the Excepted Risks as defined in clause 1.5, in which case — while the contractor must still carry out the repairs — he will be entitled to recover from the employer the cost (but not, it would seem, any profit thereon) of so doing (clause 3.3(2)).

Under clause 3.5 the contractor is made responsible both for the setting out of the Works (whether or not the engineer or someone on his behalf checks it) and for the adequacy, stability and safety of his site operations and methods of construction. This provision is essentially the same as, and covers the same ground as clauses 8(2) and 17 in the 5th Edition and, by implication, the last sentence of clause 15(2) of that form. While the legal effect is the same in both sets of conditions, the resulting responsibility placed on the contractor may in practice be heavier under the Minor Works Form in that there will seldom be a continuing presence on site by the engineer, at least at the level of expertise which is normally expected for projects subject to the 5th Edition. It is thus, if anything, somewhat more important under the Minor Works Form for the contractor to keep himself informed of events on site, as he cannot rely on the engineer's staff to pick up anything which his own staff may have missed. In particular, it is emphatically *not* the case that smaller jobs can get by with a lower level or standard of site control, rather the reverse.

UNFORESEEN CONDITIONS (CLAUSE 3.8)

During the extended consultations which preceded publication of the Minor Works Form it was argued with some force that, as the new form was intended for use only on the smaller, lower-risk projects, there was no need for the wide-ranging provisions under clause 12 of the 5th Edition which relieve the contractor of the risk of encountering unforeseen adverse physical conditions or artificial obstructions. But it was also argued with equal force that, precisely because the new form was intended for low-risk projects, any unforeseeable escalation of that risk should fall upon the employer as, unlike the situation in the building industry, all civil engineering projects were inherently vulnerable to the unexpected once the ground was opened.

In the event, it was decided that a "clause 12" provision was merited. As drafted, clause 3.8 includes the substance of clauses 12(1) to 12(4) of the 5th Edition and, save for a welcome reduction in verbiage, is with one exception of the same legal effect. The exception is that, under clause 3.8, the contractor *must* inform the engineer of each and every condition or obstruction which he thinks could not reasonably have been foreseen by an experienced contractor, whereas under the 5th Edition he is only bound to do so if he intends to make a claim for extra cost and/or an extension of time. It would seem that this extra obligation could result in a flood of minimally necessary documentation, but it must be remembered that on a 5th Edition project there will almost always be continuously on site suitably qualified representatives of the engineer who are well able to take note of site conditions as they are exposed. This is not the case on a Minor Works project and the engineer must rely on the contractor to keep him informed of all relevant site conditions; hence the difference between the two clauses.

While the express powers of the engineer set out in clause 12(2) of the 5th Edition are not included in clause 3.8 of the Minor Works form, such powers do exist elsewhere in the form. Similarly, in clause 3.8 there is no reference to the claiming or granting of extensions of time, but an express power does exist in clause 4.4(c). Finally, in both clause 12 and clause 3.8 there is provision for the contractor to be paid profit upon the extra cost occasioned by the unexpected condition or obstruction.

OTHER OBLIGATIONS UNDER CLAUSE 3

Under clause 3.9 the contractor must afford reasonable facilities for any other contractor employed by the employer and for any other properly authorised authority employed on the site. This covers the provisions of the 5th Edition clause 31(1). The express provisions of clause 31(2), of the 5th Edition, however, do not appear in the Minor Works Form, although extensions of time can be granted in suitable situations under clause 4.4(h). It follows that, when inviting tenders under the Minor Works Form, sufficient details of any other contracts that the employer has or intends to let and which might involve the contractor in providing facilities under clause 3.9 should be given, and an appropriate item included in the Schedule of Works or Bills of Quantity. It will then be open to the engineer, should the need arise, to vary the Works under clause 2.3(a) as may be appropriate and to re-value the item under clause 6.1.

As is mentioned elsewhere, it is not intended that there shall be any sub-contractors under the Minor Works Form other than "domestic" sub-contractors for whom the contractor will be entirely responsible under the ordinary law of contract. There is thus no Minor Works equivalent of the 5th Edition clauses 59A, 59B and 59C. Should the employer wish to stipulate that particular contractors (other than the contractor) shall perform specified sections of the Works he should proceed as indicated in paragraph 7 of the Notes for Guidance, which states that:-

"The Engineer may in respect of any work that is to be sub-let or material purchased in connection with the Contract list in the Specification the names of approved sub-contractors or approved suppliers of material . . ."

The Contractor's Obligations

The contractor must then select one of the sub-contractors or suppliers so named, who will then become a "domestic" sub-contractor, thereby circumventing the intractable legal difficulties of "nomination". However, the Notes for Guidance go on to say that:-

". . . *Nothing, however, should prevent the Contractor carrying out such work himself if he so chooses or from using other sub-contractors or suppliers of his own choice provided their workmanship or product is satisfactory and equal to that from an approved sub-contractor or supplier*".

Thus the employer cannot (or, at least, ought not) to have the last word in such matters. But if this is not acceptable to him, the correct course of action for the employer to adopt is to take the sub-contract or supply element out of the contract completely and to let a separate contract direct, while looking to clause 3.9 to provide for any necessary "interfacing". Of course, as between contractor and employer such action will result in the latter's bearing all the risk associated with the work or supplies thus excluded from the main contract, but that is the price to be paid for absolute choice, and one which is surely worth paying to be rid of the legal complexities and uncertainties inseparable from "nomination".

Turning now to clauses 3.6 and 3.7, the contractor is responsible for the design of temporary works unless and to the extent that the engineer may elect to take over this function. On the other hand, the contractor is not responsible for the design of the permanent Works unless the contract expressly states otherwise. In each case, the Minor Works Form reflects the principles upon which the 5th Edition is based. Moreover, as paragraph 6 of the Notes for Guidance points out:-

"*If the Contractor is required to be responsible for design work of a specialist nature which would normally be undertaken by a specialist sub-contractor or supplier (such as structural steelwire, mechanical equipment or an electrical or plumbing installation) full details must be given either in the Specification or in the Appendix to the Conditions of Contract or on the Drawings indicating precisely the Contractor's responsibility in respect of such work*".

Similarly, clause 3.6 makes the engineer responsible for the provision of any necessary instructions, drawings or other information which fall outside the scope of what the contractor ought to provide for himself as a logical consequence of his obligations under clause 3.5.

Finally, clause 3.4 requires the contractor to notify the engineer of the person duly authorised to receive instructions on behalf of the contractor. This is necessary because on a Minor Works project the contractor may have no full-time supervisor on site, just as the engineer for his part may not need to have a continuing site presence. Thus in an emergency there may be no-one on site having sufficient authority to receive instructions or take immediate action, and the engineer must know whom to contact to secure effective response to instructions. Moreover, but for this provision, and should disputes later arise, it might be difficult for the engineer or employer to prove that the contractor had received due notice of a particular instruction. Hence it is open to the contractor to ask for instructions to be delivered or sent elsewhere for the attention of his designated representative. But, as paragraph 11 of the Notes for Guidance indicates, the contractor must also accept the fact that in the interests of safety or for some other compelling reason urgent instructions may occasionally have to be given directly to the contractor's operatives on site.

STARTING AND COMPLETION (SECTION 4)

Minor Works clauses 4.1, 4.2 and 4.3 between them cover the same ground as clauses 41 and 43 and part of clause 14(1) of the 5th Edition. Thus the starting date (5th Edition "Date of Commencement of the Works") is to be either that specified in the Appendix to the Minor Works Conditions or notified by the engineer in writing, in which case it must be within a reasonable time and in any event not more than 28 days after the tender is accepted (clause 4.1). In this it differs from the 5th Edition provision which has no specified date and no prescribed limit to what the engineer (or the employer behind him) may consider to be reasonable. It follows that Minor Works tenders ought not to be accepted until it is known when the Works may proceed. However, should circumstances arise after the tender has been accepted in which the employer, for good reason, needs to postpone the start of the works for a substantial period, the problem ought not be resolved by delaying the engineer's notification (as can and does sometimes happen under the 5th Edition); either a revised starting date should be agreed with the contractor or the contract should be terminated. In either event the contractor would then have an opportunity to negotiate a suitable adjustment to his price.

The express requirement in 5th Edition clause 41 that the contractor shall proceed with the works with due expedition and without delay "in accordance with the contract" appears, slightly modified, in Minor Works clause 4.3, where the obligation is to proceed with due expedition and "reasonably in accordance with his [ie the contractor's] programme". While the Minor Works provision appears at first sight to be milder than that in the 5th Edition, common sense would suggest that the Minor Works provision probably expresses

31

what usually happens in practice under the 5th Edition. On the other hand, Minor Works clause 4.1 expressly requires the contractor to begin the works "at or as soon as reasonably possible" after the starting date, whereas the 5th Edition contains no such express term. Nevertheless, a requirement for reasonably prompt commencement will probably be implied in construing this part of the 5th Edition as a whole, so the practical effect of this apparent discrepancy is unlikely to be of any real importance.

Under both Forms of Contract the period or periods for completion of the Works must be stated in the Appendix (to the Conditions under the Minor Works Form, to the Form of Tender under the 5th Edition), and clauses 4.2 and 43 respectively are thus of identical effect. Both clauses include a reference to the provisions for extension of time.

Success in starting and finishing the Works on time logically presupposes forward planning, and the Minor Works Form follows this logic by including the submission of the contractor's programme at clause 4.3. This clause differs from 5th Edition clause 14(1) in that the submission is to be made within 14 days after the starting date which itself (under clause 4.1) may be up to 28 days after the acceptance of tender, whereas the 5th Edition requirement is for submission within 21 days of acceptance of tender. The difference may, perhaps, be explained by assuming a need under the 5th Edition for the programme to be submitted before construction starts — a need which, arguably, will not usually exist for the simpler kinds of projects likely to be carried out under the Minor Works Form. The same explanation may also serve to cover the fact that, under the Minor Works Form, the contractor need only submit his programme if asked to do so whereas, under clause 14(1), it must be submitted in any event.

A further difference is the omission from clause 4.3 of the requirement in the second sentence of clause 14(1) that the contractor "shall at the same time [as he submits his programme] also provide in writing . . . a general description of the arrangements and methods of construction" which he proposes to adopt. No such express provision appears in the Minor Works Form but, should the engineer feel that such information ought to be submitted, his power under clause 2.3(g) to give instructions for "the elucidation or explanation of any matter to enable the contractor to meet his obligations . . ." might suffice to secure an appropriate submission. On the other hand, the primary purpose of clause 2.3(g) is clearly to enable the engineer to explain the Works to the contractor and not necessarily vice-versa, so its usefulness for the purpose of securing a contractor's method statement may be open to question. In serious cases, however, suspension of progress "for the proper execution of the work" or "for the safety of the Works" can be ordered under clause 2.6(1) (a) or (b).

EXTENSIONS OF TIME

Minor Works clause 4.4 encapsulates the whole of the provisions of 5th Edition clause 44 and is essentially the same in its effect. The grounds for granting extensions of time are the same and are, moreover, set out in a manner which is far easier to read and comprehend. The Minor Works provision, however, presupposes that the contractor will first submit a request in writing for an extension, after which the engineer must grant such extension "as may in his opinion be reasonable", whereas under the 5th Edition he must assess and grant the extension to which in his opinion the contractor is fairly entitled. The test to be applied is thus somewhat less strict under the Minor Works Form but no doubt in practice engineers will take much the same view of each particular situation whichever Conditions apply.

The "three-tier" consideration under clause 44 at the initial stage, substantial completion of the Works and when the final Certificate of Completion is issued is condensed into the Minor Works provision for "regular review", as the full 5th Edition procedure is clearly inappropriate for projects which for the most part will have both started and finished well within a calendar year. The limitation in clause 44(4) that no subsequent grant shall reduce any earlier grant, however, is retained as part of the regular review under clause 4.4 and, in addition, the Minor Works Form includes a proviso that the contractor shall have taken all reasonable steps to avoid or minimise delay as a condition precedent to any grant of extension of time, which proviso is absent under the 5th Edition. This must be a definite improvement in that any refusal to proceed before a grant is made (by no means unknown under the 5th Edition) will of itself disqualify the contractor from receiving a grant under the Minor Works Form.

Before leaving the subject of extensions of time, it should be noted that there is no Minor Works provision on night and Sunday work (5th Edition clause 45) nor anything analogous to the so-called "acceleration" provisions in 5th Edition clause 46. However, for the short-duration projects for which the Minor Works Form is intended, the need for such provisions is arguably much less. Clause 45 matters can probably be handled adequately in the Specification and clause 46 matters by provision of adequate liquidated damages. Should a particular project appear to need clause 45 or 46 protection for the employer (which should be a rare situation) consideration should be given to the use of the full 5th Edition Conditions.

COMPLETION

"Substantial completion" under the 5th Edition becomes "Practical completion" under the Minor Works Form. Minor Works clause 4.5 is otherwise a commendably concise summary of the somewhat complex provisions of 5th Edition clause 48; in *intention* it is the same, and in substance it is, arguably, a great improvement. Thus clauses 4.5(1) and 4.5(2) dealing with the whole and part of the Works respectively define practical completion as occurring ". . . when the Works reach a state when notwithstanding any defect or outstanding items therein they are taken or are fit to be taken into use or possession by the employer". It follows that actual use or possession by the employer will entitle the contractor to a Certificate of Practical Completion under clause 4.5(3) whether or not such use or possession is premature and whether or not the Works would, but for that use or possession, in fact be deemed to have reached a state which would justify a Certificate.

This is clearly the right approach, as the legal effect of a clause 4.5 Certificate is now, as it should be, to vest in the employer an immediate right to possession of the Works to which the Ceritificate relates. This, in turn, is fundamental to the question of insurance and the timing of the transfer of risk from the contractor to the employer. On the other hand, it may frequently suit the employer's convenience to postpone use and possession so as to avoid the ensuing running costs, or to delay the release of retention money, or for some other non-monetary reason. While the effect of clause 48 of the 5th Edition ought to be similar, postponement under that clause is, perhaps, too easily obtained. However, under the Minor Works Form the engineer must certify practical completion (if the contractor asks for it) if in his opinion the Works are fit for take-over, whether the employer wishes it or not. Unlike clause 48, clause 4.5 is quite unambiguous on this point.

Under both Forms the engineer is not bound to certify unless the contractor requests (or, under the 5th Edition, is deemed to request) that he do so — the apparent discretion under clause 48(3) in respect of partial completion seems anomalous and, perhaps, misleading. The express 5th Edition requirement that the contractor give a written undertaking to finish outstanding work during the period of maintenance does not appear as such in the Minor Works Form but is necessarily to be implied from clause 4.7. The other difference is that under clause 48 the engineer must certify (or refuse to certify) within 21 days of the contractor's request, but under clause 4.5(3) he is only required ". . . promptly [to] certify . . . or otherwise advise the Contractor . . ." However, as the "certified date" is by definition that stated in the Certificate and not that upon which the Certificate is issued, the difference may not be of great importance unless the issue is substantially delayed (thus creating insurance difficulties for the contractor). Even then, while under the 5th Edition failure to certify within 21 days is a breach of contract entitling the contractor to damages, undue delay will clearly fail the Minor Works "promptness" stipulation and will at least hand the contractor a reasonable pretext for a claim.

Finally, the stipulation in clause 48(4) that a Certificate for sectional completion will not necessarily cover the reinstatement of ground or surfaces is missing from the Minor Works Form but, in a short project, is unlikely to be of great importance.

LIQUIDATED DAMAGES

The 65 lines of text in 5th Edition clause 47 are condensed in the Minor Works clause 4.6 into a mere 10 lines. Moreover, the complex and, in practice, seldom fully understood provisions in clause 47(2) for "sectional" damages are wholly omitted, the same effect being amply produced in a single sentence in clause 4.6. In part, this is clearly because "sectional" damages are far less likely to be needed in simple, quick projects. In those very few cases where failure to complete part of a Minor Works project on time is likely to result in disproportionately serious injury to the employer's interests, it should be quite simple to elaborate upon clause 4.6 in the Specification or even by suitably amending the Appendix to the Conditions of Contract.

Indeed, clause 47 of the 5th Edition seems already to have given rise to some particularly knotty problems of legal interpretation where the Appendix to the Form of Tender has been completed in an inconsistent manner, or even left partially completed. If and when the 5th Edition comes to be revised, it is to be hoped that some better way of meeting the problem will be devised.

Two points have not been carried over into the Minor Works Form. The first is the statement in clause 47(3) that sums payable under the clause are paid as liquidated damages and not as a penalty but, as penalties are in any event unenforceable at law (at least in England and Wales), its omission makes no difference. The second is the express power under clause 47(4) for the employer to deduct liquidated damages and the accompanying provision in clause 47(5) for their reimbursement (the latter standing or falling with clause 47(2), of course). Nothing in the Minor Works Form expressly empowers the employer to deduct, but the omission is hardly likely to cause difficulty in practice. In this connection, however, it could be argued that under Minor Works clause 7.3 the engineer should deduct liquidated damages from any certificate thereunder whereas, under the 5th Edition, it is clearly for the engineer to certify in full, leaving it to the employer to "pay short" in respect of liquidated damages. It will be interesting to see what the Courts will make of this difference should the point ever be taken there.

Finally, to complete this part of the discussion, paragraph 13(3) of the Notes for Guidance suggest a limit of liquidated damages of 10% of the estimated final contract value.

DEFECTS (SECTION 5)

"Maintenance Period" under the 5th Edition now becomes "Defects Correction Period" under the Minor Works Form. This purely semantic change is to be welcomed in that the term now accurately describes the matters with which it is concerned, namely the correction of defects after partial completion. Again, the abandonment of the term "maintenance" is probably wise in the light of the recent development of unofficial forms of contract covering works of maintenance rather than construction (eg surfacing of highways, refurbishment of sewers and the like). In this, the Minor Works Form has clearly emulated the recently-published and revised 4th Edition of the FIDIC "Civils" Conditions (the "Red Book") for the use on international contracts, where the term used is "Defects Liability Period". While this latter term is explicit enough for overseas use, the development of the English law of negligence in relation to latent defects has given it a particular legal meaning in this country, namely the "long stop" period for limitation of actions under the Latent Damage Act 1986 which is 15 years from the date of breach of contract and thus wholly different from the "maintenance period" envisaged under the ICE 5th Edition. The Minor Works' further modification to "Defects Correction Period" is thus both logical for practitioners in this country and wise.

Under the 5th Edition clause 49(1) there can be different Maintenance Periods for different sections of the Works if the engineer certifies that substantial completion took place other than on a single date.This is not so under the Minor Works Form as clause 5.1 stipulates that the Defects Correction Period (singular) shall run from the date certified as practical completion of the whole of the Works or the last period thereof. The latter arrangement seems reasonable for projects which will for the most part be of short duration. Paragraph 13(4) of the Notes for Guidance suggests that the length of the Defects Correction Period should normally be six months and in no case should exceed twelve months.

Minor Works clause 4.7 requires the contractor to complete any items

36

of work which remain outstanding at practical completion "promptly thereafter or in such manner and/or time as may be agreed or otherwise accepted by the Engineer". In addition, where parts of the Works reach practical completion early, he must maintain such parts "in the condition required by the Contract" until practical completion of the whole of the Works (fair wear and tear excepted) but not, it seems, thereafter. This differs from the generally assumed duty under the 5th Edition to continue such "maintenance" until the end of the Period of Maintenance, but it may be that this general assumption is based on a misunderstanding of 5th Edition clause 49(2) which, although less crisply drafted than the Minor Works Form, does not expressly refer to any "duty to maintain".

Minor Works clause 4.7 also includes a general duty on the contractor to rectify defects, and this is repeated in clause 5.2 for defects due to materials or workmanship not in accordance with the contract which appear during the Defects Correction Period. It should be noted that the contractor has both a duty and a right to perform such repairs, provided that he does so within a reasonable time. Thus the employer has no right to enter upon the Works (either in person or by another contractor) to remedy defects during the Defects Correction Period as, until that period has expired, the contractor has an implied discretion to manage the work to be done and may legitimately postpone repairs of early-appearing defects until he is sure that other, similar defects are not about to appear. The only exceptions to this will be if the engineer is able to order immediate rectification under some other provision of the contract (eg where the safety of the Works is involved), or if the employer gives 14 days' written notice under clause 5.3. However, the clause 5.3 provision cannot be used until the contractor has been given a reasonable time to do the work himself; what will be a reasonable time will depend upon the circumstances of each case.

Clearly, all the foregoing works of repair will normally be carried out at the contractor's own expense. However, it is arguable that, particularly where the employer has taken possession of part of the Works, defects may appear which may or may not be due to fair wear and tear. Such cases are difficult, but the better view may be that the contractor should carry out the repair even in cases of doubt and then claim reimbursement from the employer if it is not either an unfinished item or something due to sub-standard materials or workmanship. But defects appearing after the expiry of the Defects Correction Period are not covered by the foregoing provisions, and clause 5.5 makes it clear that the rights of the parties in respect of such defects remain unaffected. In particular, the contractor cannot be compelled to remedy such defects, although it may often be the most economical solution to persuade him to do so.

OTHER OBLIGATIONS

In addition to the obligations listed above, the Minor Works Form further provides as follows:-

(a) The contractor and the employer are equally bound to give effect to every instruction or decision of the engineer (clause 2.7) unless and until such instruction is altered or amended under clauses 11.3, 11.4 or 11.5.

(b) Under clause 7.2 the contractor must submit to the engineer statements of the estimated value of work completed at the end of each period of one month or longer and under clause 7.6 he must similarly submit his final account together with all supporting documentation which may reasonably be required within 28 days of the issue by the engineer of a clause 5.4 certificate.

(c) The Works must not be sub-let without the engineer's consent under clause 8.2. Where such consent is given the contractor is responsible for any acts, defaults or neglects of such sub-contractors (clause 8.3).

(d) The contractor must comply with and give all notices required by statute or byelaw and must pay any fees or charges in respect thereof (clause 9.1) subject to the exceptions set out in clause 9.3.

(e) The contractor must insure the Works (clause 10.1) and indemnify the employer as set out in clause 10.2, subject to the provisions of the remaining clauses in section 10. These arrangements conform exactly (in substance, if not wholly in form) with the requirements of clauses 20 to 25 inclusive under the 5th Edition, as otherwise probably insuperable difficulties of demarcation could arise where one contractor is carrying out work under both the 5th Edition and the Minor Works Form. However for editorial reasons the provisions of clause 20(3) "Excepted Risks" in the 5th Edition appear under "Definitions" as clause 1.5 of the Minor Works Form.

© G F Hawker 1989

CERTIFICATES AND PAYMENT

Derek Simmonds

Payment matters are dealt with under clause 7 and, in keeping with the general philosophy of the Minor Works Conditions, the rules and provisions are of a simple nature.

Clause 7.1 states that the Works are to be valued in accordance with the contract, ie in accordance with which of the five alternative bases set down in the Appendix is operative. The alternatives are:

- Lump Sum.
- Measure & Value using a priced Bill of Quantities.
- Valuation based on a Schedule of Rates (with an indication in the Schedule of the approximate quantities of major items).
- Valuation based on a Daywork Schedule.
- Cost plus fee (the cost is to be specifically defined in the contract and will exclude off-site overheads and profit).

The Appendix states that two or more bases for payment may be used on one contract, ie the work may be of such nature that part of it falls to be best dealt with on one basis whilst a different basis may be more suitable for the remainder.

Whilst this facility is available it is likely that the employer would take advantage of it on rare occasions since in so doing the intended simplicity of the contract would tend to be undermined.

When a contract is let under alternative (b) or (c) (Bill of Quantities or Schedule of Rates) the method of measurement to be employed is to be stated in the Appendix. It is to be expected that the CESMM would generally be the most appropriate document.

MONTHLY STATEMENTS

As is customary in construction contracts, the contractor submits a financial statement to the engineer at not less than monthly intervals but not necessarily at the end of each month. The facility to submit statements other than at the month end is a useful one in helping to spread the workload of both the contractor's staff and that of the engineer rather than having this concentrated about each month end.

Each monthly statement is to contain:-

● **The estimated value of work executed up to the end of the period.**

The method of estimating the value of work done will depend on the type of contract.

(i) Lump Sum

Under this method, work (other than variations) will not be measured. Hence some yardstick for payments will need to be determined in order to avoid a debate each month as to what the contractor should receive.

The contract value should, therefore, be broken down by prior agreement on an activity basis, stage basis, time scale or some other convenient method of division.

(ii) Measure & value against a Bill of Quantities

Monthly payments will be valued in the traditional way.

(iii) Valuation based on a Schedule of Rates

As with (ii) the quantities of work done will need to be ascertained. This could be done on an approximate basis to avoid the expenditure of a disproportionate amount of time to establish precise quantities each month.

There are no rules as regards attendance for measurement and it will be up to the contractor and the appointed representative of the engineer to come to an appropriate arrangement, ie whether measurement is done jointly or whether the contractor submits his measure which is then checked independently by the engineer's representative. The foregoing also applies with respect to the measurement at final account stage.

(iv) Valuation based on a Daywork Schedule

There are no stated requirements governing the submission or signing of daywork sheets or as to what the effect of a signed daywork sheet is.

The same is true as regards incidental dayworks ordered under one of the other types of contract. There, all that is required is that the contractor produces proper records and he is then paid in accordance with a Daywork Schedule included in the contract or in accordance with the Schedule of Dayworks carried out incidental to Contract Work as issued by the Federation of Civil Engineering Contractors (clause 2.5).

It is essential in both cases therefore that a suitable procedure is predetermined and the status of a signed record sheet established.

(v) Cost plus Fee

There are no provisions stating what is to be included in "cost" except, as stated in the Appendix, it excludes off-site overheads and profit. "Cost" as defined at clause 1.3 relates to cost incurred in the context of disruption or similar costs.

It is clearly necessary for tenderers to be informed as to what elements of cost will be allowed and what falls under the heading of off-site overheads.

As is common with any cost-reimbursable contract it is necessary for prior agreement to be reached as to the anticipated levels of labour and plant resources and supervision and for there to be some subsequent control over these.

● A list of goods and materials delivered to the site and their value.

In common with most standard forms, the Minor Works Conditions permit the contractor to be paid for goods delivered to site but not incorporated into the Works at the time of the preparation of a monthly statement. There is no provision for payment for materials ready but not yet delivered to site. In view of the nature of Minor Works contracts it is unlikely that this omission will create any difficulty.

● Any other items which the contractor considers should be included.

Clause 6.1 requires the engineer, after consulting with the contractor, to certify such sum as he considers fair and reasonable in respect of additional Works carried out or additional cost incurred by the contractor arising from delay or disruption to which clause 4.4 (a), (b), (d), (e) or (f) relates.

There is no requirement for a separate certificate to be issued in respect of such additional costs or indeed any other sums due on account of extra costs incurred by the contractor. Any amount determined as payable would therefore be included in the next interim certificate. An interim certificate may need to be issued after practical completion solely in respect of extra costs incurred by the contractor and agreed by the engineer, such certificate not being subject to the minimum amount restriction stated at Appendix Item 13.

Certification by the engineer and payment of monies due are to be effected within 28 days of the delivery to the engineer of each statement subject only to the restriction as to minimum value as stated at Appendix Item 13. The Guidance Notes suggest that the minimum amount of interim certificates should be 10% of the estimated final contract value rounded upwards to the nearest £1,000 but any such restriction does not apply to interim certificates issued after practical completion (clause 7.3).

An interim certificate is not conclusive as regards its accuracy and a subsequent certificate may make adjustment for any errors or omissions contained therein.

Nevertheless the engineer has a duty of care in preparing an interim certificate and may be sued if negligent certification results in loss to the employer in the event that, following over-certification and payment to the contractor, the latter became insolvent and the employer is unable to recover the excess sum paid out (See *Sutcliffe* v *Thakrah* (1974) AC 727). Certification of payment for work improperly executed may also render the engineer liable: see *Townsend* v *Stone Toms & Partners* (1984) 27 BLR 26.

VARIATIONS

A variation is a type of instruction which under clause 2.3 the engineer is empowered to issue.

Clause 2.3 (a):
"any variation to the Works including any addition thereto or omission therefrom".

Additionally in clause 2.3 (d):
"any change in the intended sequence of the Works"
would normally be considered to be a variation.

Clause 6.2 states:
"In determining a fair and resonable sum under Clause 6.1 for additional work the Engineer shall have regard to the prices contained in the Contract".

Such wording is not as restrictive as is found in other standard forms, eg "Where work is of similar character and executed under similar conditions to work priced in the Bill of Quantities it shall be valued at such rates and prices contained therein as may be applicable" (ICE Conditions of Contract, clause 52(1)) or "where work is of similar character to, is executed under similar conditions as, and does not significantly change the quantity of work set out in the Contract Bills, the rates and prices for the work so set out shall determine the Valuation" (JCT Standard Form of Building Contract, with Quantities, clause 13.5.1.1).

The more open wording of the Minor Works Form does, it is suggested, enable the engineer to take all factors into account such as the timing and relative content of the variation in reaching a fair and reasonable sum, but nevertheless the calculation thereof should not lose sight of any appropriate rate or price in the Bills of Quantities or Schedule of Rates.

Under the Lump Sum type contract the sum decided must allow for the full effect of a variation including the effect on other work unaltered in itself but affected by the variation — the consequential effect of the variation.

There is no specific reference in the Conditions in respect of those contracts where a Bill of Quantities or Schedule of Rates exists for other affected rates and prices to be adjusted so, similarly, the sum calculated in respect of the variation itself should include any consequential cost.

As regards any omission of work, clause 6.1 requires the engineer to determine "a fair and reasonable deduction".

It is only under a Lump Sum contract that there is an actual deduction on account of work omitted; in all other cases the need to deduct does not arise since only work done is valued or costed. Under a Lump Sum contract the "fair and reasonable deduction" should take into account additionally the consequential effect of the omission.

Under all other types of contract the contractor would need to make a claim under clause 6.1 if an omission in some way caused additional cost.

RETENTION

The rules regarding retention are conventional. The rate recommended in the Guidance Notes is 5% unless special circumstances warrant a different rate.

Appendix Item 12 requires a limit of retention to be set and it is recommended that in normal circumstances this should be between 2½% and 5% of the estimated final contract value.

Payment of the first release of retention is to be made within 14 days after the date of issue of the Certificate of Practical Completion and the balance within 14 days of the certificate issued under clause 5.4 when the Defects Correction Period has expired and all outstanding work and defects have been attended to (clause 7.4 and 7.5).

There are no stipulations regarding treatment of retention, ie as to its status or how the accumulated retention is to be handled prior to repayment to the contractor.

As such retention falls to be treated in accordance with the general law. Correctly, when the employer is stated to be a trustee for the contractor retention monies should be deposited in a separately identified account upon which no-one other than the employer or contractor has any claim. Thus in the event of the insolvency of the employer the contractor can, at the proper time, recover the retention that has been withheld. If nevertheless the employer has not made such special arrangements and retention monies are not separately identifiable, then despite the trust status of retention, the contractor has no claim over preferential creditors in the event of bankruptcy of the employer: see *Rayack Construction Ltd* v *Lampeter Meat Company Ltd* (1979) 12 BLR 30.

FINAL ACCOUNT

The contractor is required to submit within 28 days of the issue of the engineer's certificate under clause 5.4 (end of Defects Correction Period and clearance of defects) a final account together with all documentation reasonably necessary to enable the engineer to ascertain the final contract value and the engineer then has a further 42 days in which to do this and issue the final certificate (clause 7.6). These periods of time, though shorter than is customary under most standard forms should present no difficulty to either party in view of the simpler nature of Minor Works contracts. However, in the circumstances it would be advisable for the contractor to ascertain in advance from the engineer precisely what documentation he will require.

Within a further 14 days, that is within a total of less than 3 months from the end of physical activity on the site, the contractor should be fully paid.

Except if there has been fraud or dishonesty in respect of matters dealt with in the final certificate, it is conclusive evidence as to the sum due to the contractor under or arising out of the contract save for

Value Added Tax matters (clause 7.7) unless within 28 days of the issue of the final certificate either party has given a Notice of Dispute under clause 11.2 (the prior step to conciliation or arbitration).

With regard to all other matters the period for giving a Notice of Dispute is subject only to statute. Thus the employer is not limited to giving a Notice of Dispute regarding, say, defective work within 28 days of the final certificate but the words, "arising out of the Contract" would, it is suggested, embrace Liquidated and Ascertained Damages and hence a Notice of Dispute regarding extension of time may, by implication, be subject to the time restriction.

However, it would appear that a Notice of Dispute having been given on any matter, the conclusiveness of the final certificate as a whole is annulled. This would mean that if one party gave a Notice of Dispute on an issue within the 28 days, it could give a further Notice on another matter after the 28 days had expired even though this Notice would normally be time barred. The other party would be able to take similar advantage.

OVERDUE PAYMENTS

Clause 7.8 provides "in the event of failure of the Engineer to certify or the Employer to make payment in accordance with Contract" for the contractor to be paid interest on the amount which should have been certified or paid at 2% over the base lending rate of a bank to be specified at Appendix Item 14. Thus this provision applies to both interim payments and final payment.

Whilst the wording is suitable with respect to overdue payment of an interim certificate where an overall period, 28 days after the contractor's statement is stipulated for both certificate and payment, it would appear to be inappropriate as regards a final certificate. Here separate periods are allowed for certification and payment (42 days and 14 days respectively) and on the strict wording of the clause the contractor is said to be entitled to interest merely because the certificate is late even though payment is made in less than the 14 days and within the overall period of 56 days.

In such event the contractor will have suffered no damage as a result of the breach of contract arising from the late certification and would thus have no claim against the employer; so it is to be assumed that the drafting committeee did not intend the clause to be interpreted as suggested could be the case.

The progressive change in the law whereby a more commercial attitude now exists regarding outstanding debts is of great assistance to contractors who suffer in this respect in that it is now easier to obtain interest on the amount of an agreed debt even though the debt itself had been repaid. (See section 35A of the Supreme Court Act 1981 and section 19A of the Arbitration Act 1950 as enacted by the Administration of Justice Act 1982 and *Food Corporation of India* v *Marastro Cia Naviera SA* [1986] 3 All ER 500.

Nevertheless, the existence of a clause which establishes recovery of interest as a contractual right goes a step further in aiding creditors particularly by eliminating much legal argument which would otherwise be necessary.

VALUE ADDED TAX

Clause 7.9 is a reminder of the obligation of the employer to pay to the contractor any Value Added Tax properly chargeable on goods and services provided by the contractor. Such payment is made "notwithstanding any time for payment stipulated in the Contract". There is however no indication as to any alternative time for payment or indeed are there any detailed provisions as regards VAT liabilities of the parties, and there is no reason therefore why standard practice of the construction industry in these respects should not prevail.

© **Derek Simmonds 1989**

EXTENSIONS OF TIME AND ADDITIONAL PAYMENTS

Vincent Powell-Smith

INTRODUCTION

There is no necessary link between the provisions for extension of time for completion in clause 4.4 of the Minor Works Form and the recovery of additional payments under clause 6.1. The ICE Conditions, 5th Edition, do not provide for the recovery of prolongation or disruption costs as such, although such costs are recoverable as part of "cost" where appropriate.

Under the Minor Works Form the situation is different since clause 3.8 makes express provision for the recovery of disruption or prolongation costs as such in connection with "the delay or disruption arising" from encountering adverse physical conditions and artificial obstructions: clause 3.8. Moreover, clause 6.1 refers to the contractor incurring "additional cost *including any cost arising from delay or disruption to the progress of the Works*" as a result of specified matters (which are the fault or contractual responsibility of the employer).

For the purposes of clause 6.1, "cost" is defined (clause 1.3) as including "overhead costs whether on or off the Site of the Works *but not profit*". In contrast, under clause 3.8 the contractor is entitled not only to cost but also to "a reasonable percentage addition in respect of profit".

Although both the ICE Conditions, 5th Edition, and the Minor Works Form are quite clear about the lack of any necessary connection between the grant of an extension of time and the recovery of additional cost, it is a common misconception to suppose that for the contractor to have a monetary claim it must either be preceded by or accompanied by the determination of an extension of time. This is not so; the contractor may be granted an extension of time under clause 4.4 without his being entitled to any additional cost, eg where an extension is granted because of exceptional adverse weather under clause 4.4 (g). Conversely, he may be able to claim additional cost where the execution of the Works is disrupted by acts of the employer or of the engineer acting as his agent where there is no right to an extension of time because there is no delay to progress of the Works. In practice, of course, there is often a direct practical connection between the grant of an extension of time and the possibility of recovery of additional cost, which was a point recognised in the building contract case of *H Fairweather & Co Ltd* v *London Borough of Wandsworth* (1987) 39 BLR 106.

EXTENSIONS OF TIME

General considerations

An extension of time clause is essential in any construction contract. The liquidated damages provision (clause 4.6 and Appendix) will fail and the employer will lose his right to liquidated damages if extensions of time are not grantable under the contract *and* actually granted for any cause of delay which amounts to an act of hindrance or prevention by or on behalf of the employer: *Peak (Construction) Ltd* v *McKinney Foundations Ltd* (1970) 1 BLR 111.

On one view, therefore, the primary purpose of an extension of time clause is to preserve the employer's right to liquidated damages for the breach of late completion and to enable the employer to protect himself from the time for completion becoming "at large" because part of the delay is his fault or responsibility in law. Such a clause exists primarily to protect the employer against the possibility that some act of hindrance or prevention may disentitle him to recover liquidated damages. The secondary purpose of such a clause is, of course, to relieve the contractor from liability to pay liquidated damages because completion is delayed by some event which would otherwise be at his contractual risk.

In modern civil engineering practice the principal function of an extension of time clause is surely to enable a date to be fixed for the calculation of liquidated damages for delay, since there must be a date from which liquidated damages can run. If the contract completion date ceases to be applicable for any reason then the right to liquidated damages will be lost: *Miller v London County Council* (1934) 151 LT 425. Once lost, that right cannot be revived, leaving the employer to the inherent uncertainties of an action for general damages at common law, subject to proof of loss.

The close link between contractual provisions for liquidated damages and the grant of extensions of time was explained by Lord Justice Phillimore in *Peak v McKinney* (supra) in this way:

"[When] the parties agree that if there is delay the contractor is to be liable, they envisage that delay shall be the fault of the contractor and, of course, the agreement [for liquidated damages] is designed to save the employer from having to prove the actual damage which he has suffered. It follows, once the clause is understood in that way, that if part of the delay is due to the fault of the employer, then the clause becomes unworkable if only because there is no fixed date from which to calculate that for which the contractor is responsible and for which he must pay liquidated damages. However, the problem can be cured if allowance can be made for that part of the delay caused by the actions of the employer; and it is for this purpose that recourse is to be had to the clause dealing with extension of time. If there is a clause which provides for an extension of the contractor's time in the circumstances which happen, and if the appropriate extension is certified by the [engineer], then the delay due to the fault of the contractor is disentangled from that due to the fault of the employer and a date is fixed from which liquidated damages can be calculated".

It may also be commercially sensible to provide for the contract period to be extended for other causes of delay which are not the fault of either party, eg exceptional adverse weather, and this policy has been adopted by the draftsmen of clause 4.4 which is the provision empowering the engineer to grant an extension of time for completion in closely defined circumstances. The draftsmen have not, however, expressly addressed the problem of the grant of extensions of time retrospectively, in contrast, for example, with the extensions of time provision in another modern contract, namely the Government General Conditions of Contract for Building and Civil Engineering: GC/Works/1 — Edition 3, published in December 1989, which also prescribes an extremely sensible timetable for the award of extensions of time.

Clause 36 of that form explicitly recognises that there can be retrospective extension of time. This is probably the general rule in most cases. But from all points of view it would have been better if clause 4.4 had expressly provided for the grant of retrospective extensions of time since the case law is conflicting. In the New Zealand case of *Fernbrook Trading Co Ltd* v *Taggart* [1979] 1 NZLR 556, Mr Justice Roper took the view that, under the normal extension of time clause, a retrospective extension of time is only valid in two circumstances:

"(1) Where the cause of delay lies beyond the employer and particularly where its duration is uncertain . . . although even here it would be a reasonable inference to draw from the normal extension clause that the extension should be given a reasonable time after the factors which will govern the engineer's discretion have been established. (2) Where there are multiple causes of delay there may be no alternative but to leave the final decisions until just before the issue of the final certificate".

In another New Zealand case — *New Zealand Structures and Investments Ltd* v *McKenzie* also heard in 1979, a different judge took the view that under the normal extension of time clause the certifier can grant an extension of time right up until the time he becomes *functus officio*, ie devoid of powers, which in most cases will be on the issue of the final certificate. The court said:

"In a major contract it is virtually impossible to gauge the effect of any one cause of delay while it is still proceeding, let alone assess the consequences of concurrent or overlapping causes. Finally, any need to have a prompt decision loses some force as a factor in interpreting such a clause, when one considers the normal review and arbitration procedures . . ."

This is a realistic approach and clause 4.4 grapples with this problem by providing for a "regular review" of extensions of time granted. In some cases the argument can be put forward that the contractor is entitled to an acceleration claim where an extension of time is unreasonably delayed. This can be the case under ICE Conditions, 5th edition, and it seems also to be the situation under the Minor Works Form.

The rationale has been thus explained:
"If the contractor is driven to expedite in order to avoid possible liability for damages . . . because the engineer has failed to consider the contractor's right to an extension in good faith at the times at which he is directed to do so by clause 44, then it seems that the contractor may have a claim . . . for damages for breach of contract by the employer by way of failure of the engineer as his agent to administer

the contract in accordance with its terms": Abrahamson, **Engineering Law & the ICE Contracts**, 4th edn, p 372, citing *Morrison-Knudsen Co Inc v British Columbia Hydro Authority* (No 2) [1978] 85 DLR (3d) 186 Can.

In principle, there is no reason why such a claim should not be made under the Minor Works Form. The engineer must administer the contract fairly and in accordance with its terms and certify any extension of time promptly if it is possible to do so. If the engineer delays granting extensions and this causes the contractor to incur acceleration costs, these may be properly recoverable by way of an action for damages.

Thus, in the Australian case of *Perini Corporation Inc v Commonwealth of Australia* [1962] 2 NSWR 530 the engineer repeatedly refused to give a decision on a contractor's applications for extensions of time. The contractor accelerated in order to avoid liquidated damages and to complete on time. He was held entitled to his acceleration costs by way of damages.

It is curious that, as yet, there appear to be no reported English cases on this point, but acceleration claims are frequent in other common law countries. The difficulty would be to establish that the contractor's acceleration of the Works was the foreseeable result of the engineer's refusal to award an extension of time, especially as most liquidated damages clauses are for small figures.

Extensions of time under clause 4.4

Clause 4.4 provides:

"If progress of the Works or any part thereof shall be delayed for any of the following reasons:-

(a) an instruction given under clause 2.3 (a) (c) or (d);
(b) an instruction given under clause 2.3 (b) where the test or investigation fails to disclose non-compliance with the Contract;
(c) encountering an obstruction or condition falling within clause 3.8 and/or an instruction given under clause 2.3 (e);
(d) delay in receipt by the Contractor of necessary instructions, drawings or other information;
(e) failure by the Employer to give adequate access to the Works or possession of land required to perform the Works;
(f) delay in receipt by the Contractor of materials to be provided by the Employer under the Contract;
(g) exceptional adverse weather;

(h) other special circumstances of any kind whatsoever outside the control of the Contractor;
then provided that the Contrator has taken all reasonable steps to avoid or minimise that delay the Engineer shall upon a written request by the Contractor promptly by notice in writing grant such extension of the period for completion of the whole or part of the Works as may in his opinion be reasonable. The extended period or periods for completion shall be subject to regular review provided that no such review shall result in a decrease in any extension of time already granted by the Engineer".

Clause 4.4. is a modernised and shortened version of the traditional clause in civil engineering contracts entitling the contractor to receive from the engineer an extension of time for completion if the progress of the whole or part of the Works is delayed. At first sight, it might appear that the contractor's written request to the engineer is a condition precedent to the operation of the clause, but it is suggested that this is not the case and that the engineer is under an independent duty to grant an extension of time for completion if delay to progress is caused by one or more of the specified events although it would have been better had this been stated expressly to be the case.

In the well-known case of *London Borough of Merton* v *Stanley Hugh Leach Ltd* (1985) 32 BLR 51, the High Court had to consider whether a written notice by the contractor was a condition precedent which had to be satisfied before there was any duty on the part of the architect under a building contract in the JCT Standard Form of Building Contract, 1963 edition, to consider the grant of an extension of time. Mr Justice Vinelott rejected the view that the contractor's notice was a condition precedent to an entitlement of an extension of time, but that failure to give a notice was a breach of contract which might be taken into account by the architect in determining the extension of time. Although the wording of the relevant clause is dissimilar from that of clause 4.4, it is thought that the position must be the same, because if the contractor's notice is to be treated as a condition precedent and progress is delayed by one of the specified causes which is the employer's responsibility, then time would be "at large" and the employer would lose his right to liquidated damages.

The test to be applied by the engineer in considering the grant of an extension of time is whether "the progress of the Works or any part thereof shall be delayed" by one or more of the specified causes, ie whether the contractor is in fact held up by delay, and it is submitted that the position is the same as it is under the ICE Conditions, 5th Edition:

"The actual facts on site must be considered to determine whether the occurrence affected any operation critical to the contractor's completion time. It is not enough for the contractor to show that, according to his plans as set out in the programme, delay fell on his critical path. It is his actual not planned progress which is relevant"; Abrahamson, op cit, p139.

Case law confirms that the test is to be applied at the time the Works are actually carried out and not when they are programmed to be carried out: *Walter Lawrence & Son Ltd v Commerical Union Properties (UK) Ltd* (1984) 4 ConLR 37; *Glenlion Construction Ltd v The Guiness Trust* (1987) 11 ConLR 126.

The proviso is an important qualification to the right to an extension of time. The contractor must have taken "all reasonable steps to avoid or minimise the delay" to progress. What steps are reasonable will depend on all the circumstances, eg reprogramming may be necessary. However, it is clear that in meeting this proviso the contractor is not required to expend substantial sums of money. Obviously, there are dangers for the employer if the engineer takes a hard line where the delaying event is one which is the employer's responsibility in law. Failure by the engineer to grant an extension to which the contractor is entitled will invalidate the liquidated damages clause: *Peak v McKinney* (supra).

Eight grounds are specified as triggering off a claim for an extension of time. They are:

- Instructions requiring a variation, suspension of the whole or part of Works, or requiring any change in the intended sequence of the Works.
- Instructions requiring testing or investigation where the test or investigation fails to disclose non-compliance with the contract.
- Adverse physical conditions and obstructions and/or consequent engineer's instructions.
- Delay in receipt by the contractor of necessary drawings, instructions or other information from the engineer.
- Failure of the employer to give adequate access to the Works or possession of land required to perform them.
- Delayed receipt of materials to be provided to the contractor by the employer under the contract.
- Exceptional adverse weather. Normal bad weather is at the contractor's risk.
- Other special circumstances of any kind whatsoever outside the control of the contractor.

This last sweeping-up ground is important. What "other special circumstances" are will depend on the interpretation of the contract as a whole. In contrast to the position under the ICE Conditions, 5th

Edition, the words "outside the control of the contractor" have been added, presumably because general words such as "other special circumstances of any kind whatsoever" will not be interpreted as enpowering the engineer to grant an extension for delay due to the employer's default and are to be restrictively construed: *Peak v McKinney* (Supra).

If progress of the Works (or part of them) is delayed because of the happening of one or more of these events, the engineer is bound "upon a written request by the contractor *promptly* by notice in writing grant such extension of the period for completion . . . as may in his opinion be reasonable" (italics supplied). No particular form of request is specified, except that it must be in writing, but it is in the contractor's interest to provide the engineer with as much relevant information as possible; and the engineer is entitled to seek further information from the contractor if this is necessary.

As indicated earlier, it is not thought that the contractor's notice is a condition precedent to the grant of an extension of time, and if the engineer becomes aware that progress of the whole or part of the Works is delayed because of an event falling within clause 4.4, it is suggested that he must grant an appropriate extension of time, whether or not the contractor has made a written request to him. He should do this before the current date for completion of the Works (or the appropriate part of them) has passed — certainly if the delay is the responsibility of the employer.

In the normal case, of course, the contractor will make a written request for an extension to the engineer. The engineer must then consider it and assess any extension of time which is merited, and notify the contractor in writing of any extension granted. The wording of the clause clearly prohibits the very common practice of postponing consideration of extensions of time until the end of the contract; the extension must be granted *promptly* upon receipt of the claim.

It should be noted that there is no mechanism for allocating extensions of time between different heads: see *H Fairweather & Co Ltd v London Borough of Wandsworth* (1987) 39 BLR 106, rejecting the view that where delaying events occur which cause delay and which can be ascribed to more than one of the reasons set out in an extension of time clause, then the extension must be granted for the "dominant" reason.

The engineer is also under a duty to subject "the extended period or periods for completion . . . to regular review", but his regular review cannot decrease any extensions already granted. The engineer's duty is to look at contract progress on a periodic basis and to keep the situation under review.

Nothing is said about the circumstances which the engineer must take into account in assessing what extensions to grant. There are no defined criteria except that the progress of the whole or part of the Works must be delayed and the extension granted is to be one which, in the engineer's opinion, is "reasonable". Clearly, however, the engineer must have regard to such things as omissions and may take into account any delay which is caused by the contractor himself.

The extension to be granted is one which is reasonable in the opinion of the particular engineer. Within limits, this is a personal decision, and different engineers might well reach slightly different conclusions on the same facts. The granting of extensions of time is not an exact science. The engineer is, of course, under a duty to act fairly and impartially, and the reasonableness of the engineer's decision can be challenged under the disputes procedure. Clause 11.7 confers on the arbitrator "full power to open up, review and revise any decision, instruction, certificate or valuation of the engineer" and in effect to substitute his own opinion for that of the engineer.

ADDITIONAL PAYMENTS UNDER CLAUSE 6

Most construction contracts provide machinery for dealing with monetary claims arising as the Works proceed, and the ICE Minor Works Form is no exception. Clause 6.1 provides, *inter alia*, for money claims by the contractor based on additional cost which, for the purposes of the sub-clause, excludes profit. Claims for adverse physical conditions and artificial obstructions are dealt with separately by clause 3.8. In the case of additional work, etc, in a clause 3.8 situation, the contractor is entitled to cost plus a reasonable percentage addition for profit; but he is entitled only to "additional cost" in respect of any resultant delay or disruption.

Clause 6.1. is the general "claims" provision and provides: "If the Contractor carries out additional Works or incurs additional cost including any cost arising from delay or disruption to the progress of the Works as a result of any of the matters referred to in paragraphs (a) (b) (d) (e) or (f) of clause 4.4 the Engineer shall certify and the Employer shall pay to the Contractor such additional sum as the Engineer after consultation with the Contractor considers fair and reasonable. Likewise the Engineer shall determine a fair and resonable deduction to be made in respect of any omission of work".

This important provision covers not only additional work (see clause 6.2 as to valuation) but also additional cost incurred by the contractor "including any cost arising from delay or disruption to the progress of the Works" as a result of specified matters. These are:

- Variation instructions: clause 2.3(a).
- Instructions requiring suspension of the whole or part of the Works: clause 2.3(c).
- Instructions changing the intended sequence of the Works: clause 2.3(d).
- Instructions requiring testing and investigation where the test or investigation does not disclose non-compliance with the contract: clause 2.3(b).
- Delayed receipt by the contractor of necessary instructions, drawings or other information: clause 4.4(d).
- Employer's failure to give adequate access to the Works or possession of land required for their performance: clause 4.4(e).
- Delayed receipt by the contractor of materials to be provided by the employer under the contract: clause 4.4(f).

Only these matters give rise to a contractual claim and to reimbursement under the contract provisions, and it is only these claims which the engineer has power to deal with. Clause 6.1 is not exhaustive of the contractor's remedies since he may elect to pursue a claim at common law if the event relied on amounts to a breach of contract, eg delay by the engineer in supplying necessary drawings, instructions or information. There is also the possibility of a claim for breach of an implied term of the contract, but such claims would have to be dealt with in arbitration.

The procedure under clause 6.1 is refreshingly simple, since there are no complicated notice procedures or restrictive conditions, the engineer is to certify additional cost payments "if the Contractor . . . incurs additional cost including any cost arising from delay or disruption to the progress of the Works as a result of any of the" specified matters. He is to do this "after consultation with the contractor" and the only practical issue is what sum the engineer considers "fair and reasonable".

It is quite clear that the contractor must provide the engineer with particulars and details of the additional costs incurred, since the engineer cannot determine what is a "fair and reasonable" additional sum in a vacuum. Figures cannot be plucked out of the air and the settlement is to be made on the basis of actual cost.

All the grounds of claim covered by clause 6.1 have in common the entitlement of the contractor to cost only. This is defined (clause 1.3) as including "overhead costs whether on or off the Site of the Works but not profit". However, the Conditions do not exclude the contractor's right to claim damages at common law if the act relied on amounts to a breach of contract, and in a prolongation situation where the contractor can establish that had it not been for the delay he might have been engaged on other profitable work elsewhere, it might well be in his interests to pursue his alternative claim at common law.

For the principles of claims assessment, reference may be made to **Civil Engineering Claims** by Vincent Powell-Smith and Douglas Stephenson, BSP Professional Books, London, 1989.

CLAIMS FOR ADVERSE PHYSICAL CONDITIONS ETC

One of the most prolific sources of contractors' claims — the encountering of adverse physical conditions and artificial obstructions — is dealt with separately by clause 3.8. This provides:

"If during the execution of the Works the Contractor shall encounter any artificial obstruction or physical condition (other than a weather condition or a condition due to weather) which obstruction or condition could not in his opinion have been foreseen by an experienced contractor the Contractor shall as early as practicable give written notice thereof to the Engineer. If in the opinion of the Engineer such obstruction or condition could not reasonably have been foreseen by an experienced contractor then the Engineer shall certify and the Employer shall pay a fair and reasonable sum to cover the cost of performing any additional work or using any additional plant or equipment together with a reasonable percentage addition in respect of profit as a result of:-

● complying with any instructions which the Engineer may issue; and/or
● taking proper and reasonable measures to overcome or deal with the obstruction or condition in the adsence of instructions from the Engineer; together with such sum as shall be agreed as the additional cost to the Contractor of the delay or disruption arising therefrom. Failing agreement of such sums the Engineer shall determine the fair and reasonable sum to be paid".

Clause 3.8. is a simplified and more straightforward version of its parent in the ICE Conditions, 5th Edition, and is similar in its approach, although the engineer's power to give instructions to deal with the problem is more widely cast.

The little case law that has arisen under clause 12 of the 5th Edition is of relevance in clause 3.8 and thus clause 3.8 is not limited to supervening events: *Holland Dredging (UK) Ltd v Dredging & Construction Co Ltd* (1987) 14 ConLR 30. The principle of the clause is that the cost of dealing with unforeseeable physical conditions or artificial obstructions should be borne by the employer and it alters the position at common law. It is therefore for the contractor to bring his claim within the words of clause 3.8. No guidance is given as to the meaning to be attributed to "physical conditions" or "artificial obstructions" but the exclusion of " a weather condition or a condition due to weather" is important. Temporary physical conditions are, it is thought, within the provision while it is plain that in this context "artificial obstructions" must have a physical connotation.

The main limitation is that the obstruction or condition must be one which "could not reasonably have been foreseen by an experienced contractor" and the burden of establishing that this is so lies on the contractor.

In *C J Pearce & Co Ltd* v *Hereford Corporation* (1968) 66 LGR 647, a case arising under the 4th Edition of the ICE Conditions, the contractors knew before tender that an old sewer had to be crossed, and a map supplied to all tenderers showed its "approximate line" which was accepted to be accurate within 10 to 15 feet on either side. The old sewer was fractured when the contractors were building a new one. The court held that the obstruction could have been reasonably foreseen and that the contractors had no claim. An experienced contractor should have foreseen a substantial risk in light of the information available to him and this appears to be the test which must be applied.

Under clause 3.8. the contractor's duty is to give a written notice whenever he encounters *any* artificial obstruction or physical condition during the execution of the Works which he thinks could not have reasonably been foreseen by an experienced contractor and this is couched as a general obligation. This notice must be served "as early as possible" after encountering the obstruction or condition and notice sooner rather than later is essential. Not only is the contractor's notice a condition precedent to any right of recovery of extra cost, but it is also to ensure that the engineer is forewarned: *J Crosby & Sons Ltd* v *Portland Urban District Council* (1967) 5 BLR 121; *Hersent Offshore SA* v *Burmah Oil Tankers Ltd* (1978) 2 Lloyds Rep 565.

If the engineer forms the opinion that the obstruction or condition could not have been reasonably foreseen by an experienced contractor, then he is to determine and certify a fair and reasonable sum (including a reasonable percentage for profit) to cover the cost of carrying out the necessary additional work etc, as a result of the contractor's compliance with any instructions given by the engineer to overcome the problem and/or the contractor having taken proper and reasonable measures to deal with the problem in the absence of an instruction from the engineer.

The contractor is also entitiled to "such sum as shall be agreed as the additional cost to the contractor" of any resultant disruption and delay. No profit is allowable on this element of the claim. Failing agreement, it is for the engineer to determine the amount to be paid; it is to be a "fair and reasonable sum". The engineer's decision is reviewable in arbitration and obviously it is for the contractor to provide substantiating evidence to support any claim which he wishes to make.

The wording of the clause does not restrict payment to costs incurred after the giving of notice by the contractor. However, the contract is silent as to what is "a reasonable percentage addition in respect of profit". It is thought that the contractor's own profit levels on the actual contract should be used as a starting point, but they are not necessarily decisive.

Encountering an obstruction or condition covered by clause 3.8 also gives rise to a claim for extension of time under clause 4.4 (c).

© **Vincent Powell-Smith 1989**

PROCEDURE FOR DISPUTES

John Uff

INTRODUCTION

The ICE Conditions of Contract for Minor Works broke new ground in terms of contracts produced by the Institution. Previous editions of the ICE 5th Edition Main Works Form and the Form of Contract for Ground Investigation all followed the same format, with the same clause numbers dealing with the same subjects. The Minor Works Form, for the first time, started with a clean sheet, with no preconceived notions as to the necessary numbers of clauses, the arrangement of subject matter nor, most important of all, the procedures which were going to be built into the contract. In regard to disputes, this led to a radically different approach from that contained in most other forms of engineering contract.

The ICE Main Works Form, in common with the Ground Investigation Form, the derivative FIDIC Form, as well as other less closely related engineering forms, all use a two-stage disputes procedure involving an initial reference to the engineer, which is usually expressed as a condition precedent to the right to arbitration upon the engineer's decision. Experience indicates that this procedure is regarded as cumbersome, and on occasions, a serious impediment to a party wishing to have a bona fide dispute properly dealt with under the contract. During the drafting stage of the Minor Works Form, the possibility of other means of dispute resolution was discussed at two public meetings at the Institution of Civil Engineers, from which it appeared that there was a sizeable body of opinion within the membership which was prepared to consider alternatives. The particular alternative advocated for a number of years by the Federation of Civil Engineering Contractors was conciliation. This new form appeared to be the right opportunity to try this alternative procedure. Accordingly, the contract as now printed provides two major departures from the Main Works Form. First, there is no provision for reference to the enigneer; and secondly, there is an optional right to conciliation in advance of formal arbitration. The relevant provisions are contained in clause 11 of the new form.

In common with other standard forms, the provisions for arbitration must now be read in the light of the Court of Appeal decision in the *Northern Regional Health Authority* v *Derek Crouch Construction Co Ltd* [1984] QB 644 and other decisions on the topic, most recently the decision of H H Sir William Stabb in *J F Finnegan Ltd* v *Sheffield City Council* (1988) 43 BLR 124. The effect of these decisions is that, if the parties take their dispute to Court, the judge will not be able to exercise the powers and jurisdiction which are given to the arbitrator under the contract. This principle, as now interpreted in subsequent decisions including the *Finnegan* case has the effect that the arbitration clause is not to be read as disenabling the Court, but rather as enabling the arbitrator to exercise the powers set out. Consequently, if any matters arise in respect of which the arbitrator is not empowered to act, there may be no right to maintain a dispute at all. And of more practical importance, if the parties by deletion or separate agreement, seek to remove the requirement for arbitration, they must ensure that the Court will in fact be vested with jurisdiction over the matters in question.

OUTLINE OF DISPUTE PROCEDURE

The dispute procedure under the Minor Works Form is contained in clause 11 of the Conditions of Contract, together with the Institution of Civil Engineers' Conciliation Procedure (1988) and the Incorporated ICE Arbitration Procedure (1983) Part F (Short Procedure). The Conciliation Procedure is published with and included in the printed form, but the Arbitration Procedure must be obtained separately. Note that both the Conciliation Procedure and the Arbitration Procedure refer to any amendments or modifications that may be in force, respectively, at the date of the Notice of Dispute or appointment of the arbitrator. At the time of going to press, there are no amendments to either document, but amendments to the ICE

Arbitration Procedure are to be anticipated in the light of various amendments which have taken place to the ICE Conditions of Contract since 1983, and also in view of possible changes in English arbitration law indicated by the recent report of the Mustill Committee (September 1989).

The operation of the disputes procedure under the Minor Works Form, in outline, commences with a Notice of Dispute to be served by the party wishing to initiate the dispute process (clause 11.2). This notice is required whether the party giving it intends to proceed by conciliation or arbitration or both. Thereafter, within 28 days of service of the Notice of Dispute, either party may give notice requiring either conciliation (clause 11.3) or arbitration (clause 11.5). If conciliation is pursued, then within 28 days of receipt of the conciliator's recommendation, either party may refer the matter to arbitration. The arbitration is to be conducted in accordance with the short procedure under the ICE Arbitration Procedure. However, the decision of the conciliator will become binding if no notice of arbitration is given within the required period of 28 days (clause 11.4).

NOTICE OF DISPUTE

Clause 11.2 makes provision for service of a Notice of Dispute, upon which the dispute is deemed to arise. The provisions are procedural rather than substantive, but the clause provides usefully that no Notice of Dispute may be served unless the party serving the notice has taken steps available under the contract regarding the dispute and the other party or the engineer has either (a) taken any steps required of him or (b) been allowed reasonable time. This is a useful safeguard against premature raising of disputes.

In theory, there could be a dispute about whether a Notice of Dispute could be served, on the basis that the pre-requisites are not satisfied. This could be so, eg where the employer has not finally rejected a claim by the contractor. There could also be an objection on wider grounds, eg that the contractor has not provided sufficient details of the claim and the engineer and/or employer have not been able to consider it. Ultimately, such matters could affect the jurisdiction of an arbitrator, and the enforceability of his Award. In any such case, the arbitrator should seek to establish agreement between the parties that a dispute has arisen and that he is properly appointed to deal with it. In the case of conciliation, the question of jurisdiction is of less importance, because the process has to be consensual.

However, a point could still arise if it were subsequently contended that the Conciliator's opinion had become final under clause 11.4.

The Notice of Dispute is of particular relevance in regard to the Final Certificate referred to in clause 7.7. This certificate is to be "conclusive evidence as to the sum due to the Contractor under or arising out of the Contract . . . unless either party has within 28 days after the issue of the Final Certificate given notice under Clause 11.2" (the only exception relates to VAT). If the Final Certificate has been given, then it may be taken that the engineer or the other party has by that stage taken any steps that may be required of him in relation to the dispute.

POSITION OF THE ENGINEER

The contract provides for appointment of a "named individual" to act as engineer. This provision was regarded as controversial, in the light of the debate under the ICE Main Form of Contract, as to whether it is acceptable for the engineer to be a firm or, as is often the case now, a limited company. Strong views have been expressed on both sides. In regard to the Minor Works Form, however, the draftsmen took the view that the limited nature of the works was such that it would always be more appropriate to have an identified individual. Clause 2.1, as well as providing for the engineer's appointment, also provides for his replacement as necessary, so that the employer is not bound to retain the same person throughout.

The engineer is given extensive and specific powers to give instructions (clause 2.3) and is required to carry out the usual functions of administration and certification under the contract. The engineer is not given any function in regard to disputes in the way provided for under Clause 66 of the ICE 5th Edition Main Form of Contract, or under other derivatives such as clause 67 of the FIDIC Form of Contract. Clause 2.4 of the Minor Works Form, however, does provide a limited right of appeal to the engineer. The clause provides for the engineer, resident engineer or other delegated person to specify at the request of the contractor the provision under which any particular instruction has been given. The clause goes on to provide that if the contractor shall be satisfied "with any such instruction, he shall be entitled to refer the matter to the engineer for his decision." It may be that this provision was intended to apply only in circumstances where the contractor was dissatisfied with the answer given regarding the authority to give an instruction. However, the clause appears to entitle the contractor to challenge any instruction, on its merits and not simply on the authority to give the instruction. The engineer, may, thus, be requested to review his own instruction in the same way as provided under clause 66 of the Main ICE Form. However, no consequence appears to flow either from the decision of the engineer on such a reference, or from the failure of the contractor to make such a reference. The clause is, in effect, simply a way of giving the engineer an opportunity to confirm (or otherwise) instructions. If the contractor has referred certain instructions to the engineer under clause 2.4, it would follow that he cannot serve a Notice of Dispute in relation to the same matters until the engineer has had a reasonable time to give his decision.

Once the engineer has made his decision on any claim that may be submitted by the contractor (or by the employer) he ceases to have any further function in relation to those matters, except to the limited extent of a challenge under clause 2.4. Thereafter, if the matter is referred under clause 11 either to conciliation or arbitration, the engineer remains a competent and compellable witness. He may, of course, be called by either side although it would usually fall to the employer to invite the engineer to give evidence, and the engineer's term of engagement may expressly require him to provide assistance in any subsequent dispute that may arise. In regard to conciliation, the conciliator is not bound by the normal rules of evidence (which prevent arbitrators from themselves calling witnesses) and the conciliator would certainly have the power to interview the engineer separately from either of the parties. It would normally be anticipated that the conciliator would wish to avail himself of this opportunity.

THE OPTION OF CONCILIATION

Clause 11.3 allows either party within 28 days after service of the Notice of Dispute under clause 11.2, to give notice in writing requiring the dispute to be referred to conciliation. Such notice may not be given, however, if a Notice to Refer under clause 11.5 (to arbitration) has already been served. Thus, it is up to the two parties to decide whether they wish to arbitrate or conciliate, and the first notice served will normally prevail. However, it should be noted that conciliation is essentially consensual. It relies on a degree of co-operation and the conciliator's opinion is not binding. Consequently, if a difference arises as to whether the original dispute should be referred to conciliation or arbitration, there is little point in one party insisting on conciliation if the other side appears determined to arbitrate. Nevertheless, it must be likely that the act of one party preferring conciliation would at least incline the other party to give serious consideration to it.

What is conciliation? The contract itself does not provide an answer, but requires the process to be conducted under the Institution of Civil Engineers' Conciliation Procedure (1988) or any amendment thereof being in force at the date of the notice requiring conciliation. The process as defined in the procedure is intended to produce a form of non-binding "decision" or finding on the disputes. It is not simply a process of ascertaining the views of the parties in order to find common ground between them (sometimes called mediation). The essence of conciliation as provided for under this contract is that the conciliator gives an independent view of the diputes, subject obviously to the limitations of the conciliation process itself. The fact that the process is intended to produce something in the nature of a "decision" is emphasised by the provision in clause 11.4 which renders the recommendation of the conciliator binding as a settlement of the dispute where Notice of Arbitration is not given within 28 days of receipt of the recommendation.

THE ICE CONCILIATION PROCEDURE

This is set out in the form of printed rules which are included as a loose leaf insert with the contract. Rule 2 provides that the rules are to be interpreted and applied in the manner most conducive to the efficient conduct of the proceedings with the primary objective of obtaining the conciliator's recommendations as quickly as possible. This is backed up by explicit time limits, particularly an overall limit of 2 months from appointment under Rule 6.

Explicit time limits appear in a number of rules. Thus, Rule 8 limits the period allowed for receiving further written submissions (after the initial service of written submissions) to 14 days. Rule 12 (1) requires the conciliator to prepare his recommendations within 21 days of the conclusion of any meeting held under Rule 10; and if the conciliator is to give an opinion (presumably giving reasons) in addition to his recommendations, he must do so within 7 days of giving his recommendations. Such express time limits will in the ordinary way be of little consequence, since the conciliator's recommendations become binding only if the parties agree. However, in the event of the recommendations becoming binding pursuant to clause 11.4, then it may be anticipated that the party adversely affected thereby would seek to show that the "conciliator's decision" was *ultra vires*, or otherwise without jurisdiction, and one way of doing this would be to show that the conciliator had gone outside mandatory time rules without agreement. While the parties may often be taken to waive any such objection, the conciliator should, in the interests of finality, ensure that any extension of time is agreed to and noted accordingly.

Particular features of the conciliation procedure to be noted are the following:

Rule 3 provides for Notice in writing to be given, accompanied by a brief statement of the matters for conciliation and the relief or remedy sought. Note that the rules provide for the parties to have an opportunity of making further written submissions under Rules 7 and 8 and oral submissions if a meeting is convened under Rule 10.

Rule 4 provides for appointment of a conciliator by agreement within 14 days of notice under Rule 3, or in default by the President or a Vice President of the ICE. The appointment of a conciliator actually agreed by the parties is obviously desirable since the parties have to agree to accept his recommendation. However, if this is not possible and there is an appointment through the ICE, the parties will at least have the benefit of knowing that the coinciliator appointed will be a person of known experience and suitability in this type of work.

Rule 7 provides that the parties may serve written submissions including written statements of evidence. The written submission is to be accompanied by relevant documents relied on. There is no provision for discovery of documents in the possession of the other party, so that the submission will usually refer only to documents which assist the party's case, or to adverse documents which are in the possession of the other party, and likely to be relied on.

Rule 8 allows the conciliator to receive further written submissions in reply. These submissions are required to be for the purpose of "replying specifically to points made in any other party's original submission"; but a party could not be prevented from making wider submissions, and it would be a matter for the conciliator's discretion whether he took them into account.

Rule 9 gives the conciliator wide powers in investigating the dispute. These permit him to inform himself about the nature and facts of the dispute "in any way he thinks fit" including meeting the parties separately. This is an important power which virtually gives the conciliator carte blanche in regard to the material he obtains and considers.

Rule 10 allows (but does not require) the conciliator to hold a meeting where he may receive evidence without being bound by the rules of evidence. Thus, he is under no obligation to permit cross-examination, and he may hear and act on hearsay evidence.

Rule 12 deals with the product of the conciliation. This is referred to as the conciliator's "recommendation" which appears to be intended as a statement of the recommended outcome of the dispute, eg which party should pay how much to the other. Where there are multiple claims, there is no obligation to deal with them separately, and the conciliator could simply recommend a global figure in settlement of all the disputes. Sub-Rule 2 provides for the service of a separate "written opinion", which is to contain reasons and comments as the conciliator deems appropriate. Sub-Rule 3 expressly empowers the conciliator to give preliminary views, ie he would not disqualify himself (as an arbitrator might) by expressing views and "entering the fray" or involving himself in the dispute.

The conciliator is given, under the rules, wide powers to investigate and form his opinion about the dispute. In addition to the specific powers set out in the rules, he is given a general power to seek legal or "other advice" (Rule 11). The latter may presumably include technical advice on any matter which the conciliator does not feel competent to deal with. The conciliator's fees are normally to be paid half by each part (Rule 13). Unless the parties otherwise agree, the conciliator may not thereafter be appointed arbitrator (Rule 14).

POWERS AND DUTIES OF THE CONCILIATOR

Since the conciliation is a comparatively new field and since flexibility is clearly of the essence, it is to be expected that the conciliator will need comparatively wide powers and correspondingly few duties. As the parties are not ordinarily bound by the result, it would be to little purpose to permit procedural objections.

The duties of the conciliator are to start the conciliation as soon as possible after appointment and to conclude within 2 months (Rule 6) subject to any extension the parties may agree. If the conciliator holds a meeting with the parties then he becomes under a further duty (which may apparently shorten the overall time scale) to prepare his recommendations within 21 days of the conclusion of such meeting (Rule 12 (1)).

The powers and discretion given to the conciliator are considerable. If the parties avail themselves of the opportunity to send written submissions or statements to the conciliator under Rule 7, the conciliator then has a discretion whether to allow further written submissions in reply within a futher 14 days (Rule 8). Whether or not there are to be written submissions, the conciliator may at any time on giving at least 24 hours notice, visit and inspect the site or the subject matter of the dispute, and he may inform himself in any way he thinks fit about the dispute, including the express right to meet the parties separately (Rule 9).

The conciliator is given power to convene a meeting with both parties on giving not less than 7 days notice (unless the parties agree a shorter period). When taking evidence or hearing submissions the conciliator is not to be bound by the rules of evidence or by any other rules or procedure (Rule 10). The conciliator is also given complete discretion to seek legal or other advice (Rule 11) which will be at the expense of the parties. Upon giving his recommendations for settlement, the conciliator has a discretion to give, either with his recommendations or separately, a written opinion including reasons or comments (Rule 12 (2)).

Rule 13 is designed to give the conciliator an express lien over his recommendation against payment of his fees. While this is a right which would be available to the conciliator under the general law, it is questionable how the exercise of such lien would affect the duty of the conciliator to conclude the conciliation within 2 months of appointment (Rule 6) and within 21 days of any meeting with the parties (Rule 12 (1)). Where time is at a premium, it is obviously undesirable to create any risk that the programme will be held up for payment of fees. Conciliators would be better advised to ensure that adequate security for their fees is provided in advance, for example, in the form of a deposit or a solicitor's undertaking.

ARBITRATION AND THE ICE PROCEDURE

Arbitration is available directly under clause 11.5 of the Conditions where the dispute has not first been referred to conciliation under clause 11.3. Note that clause 11.5 provides that where Notice to Refer is not served within 28 days of Notice of Dispute, the latter notice is deemed to have been withdrawn. This provision may have the most serious consequenes in relation to a Final Certificate, the finality of which has been challenged by notice properly given under clause 11.2 (see above).

Arbitration is also available after conciliation. Under clause 11.4, either party may within 28 days after receipt of the conciliator's recommendation refer the dispute to arbitration by written Notice to Refer. Note that where such notice is not given within this period the recommendation of the conciliator is deemed to have been accepted in settlement of the dispute. There can be no doubt that the court would incline strongly to uphold the finality of conciliation in such circumstances, following cases such as *P & M Kay Ltd* v *Hosier & Dickinson Ltd* [1972] 1 All ER 121, subject only to the possibility of being granted an extension of time pursuant to section 27 of the Arbitration Act 1950. Such an extension is, however, granted only in exceptional circumstances such as where one party has been misled in his appreciation of his rights.

A dispute which proceeds to arbitration under the ICE Minor Works Form is required to follow the Short Procedure in part F, unless the parties otherwise agree in writing. This Short Procedure has, since the inception of the 1983 Arbitration Procedure proved popular for the resolution of small to medium disputes, and occasionally for substantial disputes. The parties and arbitrators who have used this procedure are reportedly generally encouraged by the efficiency, speed and comparatively low cost of the procedure, qualities which appear elusive in other forms of arbitration.

The essence of the Short Procedure, Part F, is that the arbitration commences with each party setting out his case in a document or file containing (Rule 20.2):

(a) a statement as to the Orders or Awards he seeks;
(b) a statement of his reasons for being entitled to such Orders or Awards;
(c) copies of documents relied on (including statements) identifying the origin or date of each.

The procedure does not state whether this exchange of cases should be simultaneous or sequential, this being a matter for the arbitrator to decide, usually at an initial procedural meeting. The arbitrator, after reading the parties' cases may require further documents or information (Rule 20.3). Within one month of receiving these documents, the arbitrator is to fix a hearing of one day (or longer if required) for the purpose of receiving oral submissions and/or questions being put by the arbitrator (Rule 20.4). Thereafter the arbitrator is to make his Award within a further one month.

Rule 21.1 of the Short Procedure provides that the arbitrator is to have no power to award costs to either party and the arbitrator's fees and charges are to be paid by the parties in equal shares. When originally included in the ICE Arbitration Procedure, this provision was unobjectionable, because the Short Procedure itself required specific agreement of the parties to the particular rules. Under the Minor Works Form, however, the Short Procedure is made mandatory, unless otherwise agreed by the parties (ie the parties can agree to arbitrate in accordance with any other procedure, or other parts of the ICE procedure). Strictly, a provision made in advance of a dispute arising that the parties shall in any event pay their own costs, is rendered void by section 18 (3) of the Arbitration Act 1950. Such an agreement has to be made after the dispute has arisen. This would still leave the arbitrator with power to deal with the costs in his discretion, and it may be that he could take into account the fact that the parties had entered into a form of contract providing, in effect, that they would pay their own costs. However, a safer course is for the arbitrator, at the outset, to invite the parties to confirm their agreement that he shall have no power to award costs (in effect requiring the parties to pay their own costs).

STATUS OF CONCILIATION IN ARBITRATION

One matter which is of potential concern to the parties and particularly to conciliators, is the role, if any, which the conciliation and indeed the conciliator himself, may play in any subsequent arbitration. The conciliation documents are not privileged and may well be regarded as directly relevant to the arbitration. Indeed, it would be unrealistic to suppose that an arbitrator subsequently appointed will not, by one means or another, become aware of the proceedings and the results of any attempted conciliation. It is not thought, however, that this should be regarded as any disadvantage to the proper conduct of the proceedings. At worst, it will create an apparent onus of proof on the party who seeks to overturn the view of the conciliator and achieve a more favourable result in the arbitration.

One matter of some practical consequence is the position of the conciliator personally. There is no reason in principle why he should not be required to give evidence before the arbitrator, in the same way that an engineer who has himself made a decision on a dispute before arbitration is a competent and compellable witness. Two problems may arise in relation to the conciliator. First, he may be reluctant to be further involved in the dispute. It is by no means clear how and by whom he would be paid for any further services required of him. Secondly, a more fundamental difficulty lies in the nature of any evidence which the conciliator might give. His testimony as to the facts will *ex hypothesi* be hearsay, but this would be no reason to reject his evidence as an opinion ranking with other expert evidence.

It may well be that the solution to both of these problems lies in the practical question of who would wish to call the conciliator as a witness. In general, an arbitrator cannot call a witness himself. The party wishing to challenge the opinion of the conciliator will not call him because he would be bound by the conciliator's evidence. The opposing party, who might be tempted to call the conciliator to support his own case, is unlikely to do so, since this will give the opposing party the opportunity to cross-examine. The practical result, it is thought, is that conciliators personally are unlikely to be troubled to participate in subsequent arbitration. The documents they produce, however, are likely to figure but it will be for the parties and the subsequent arbitrator to make the best that they can of them.

CONCILIATOR AS ARBITRATOR

One final provision in the conciliation rules is that the conciliator is not to be appointed arbitrator in any subsequent dispute arising out of the same contract unless the parties otherwise agree in writing (Rule 14). This obviously sensible provision may be seen as legislating against the highly unlikely, but it may also serve to draw to the parties' attention the possibility that they might make such an agreement, eg where one party is only marginally dissatisfied with the conciliation, possibly on the ground that the conciliator has not given full weight to or has not had time to understand his case. There will undoubtedly be some instances in which parties will be tempted to "continue" with the conciliation in the guise of arbitration, but before the same individual as tribunal. Where this is contemplated the parties should bear in mind a number of difficulties that will need to be resolved including the following:

- The parties will be bound by the award given in the arbitration.
- Notice to refer under clause 11.4 must still be given, otherwise the conciliation will become binding.
- The conciliator, upon becoming an arbitrator, must adopt the rules of conduct applicable to arbitration, which will be considerably tighter than those applying under the conciliation rules.
- The parties must agree and record the extent to which the conciliator may treat information obtained in the course of the conciliation as having also been obtained for the purpose of the arbitration.
- The parties must also decide and record whether and to what extent they are to revert to the strict rules applicable in arbitration, eg the rules of evidence, and how evidence already received which did not comply with these rules is to be dealt with (eg information received from one party in the absence of the other).

These difficulties are not insurmountable but they are formidable. An alternative and probably perferable course, after delivery of the conciliator's recommendations, would be to agree expressly to extend the conciliation by agreement that the existing recommendation should not become binding and that (for example) the process of conciliation should continue until such time as either party serves notice on the other requiring the conciliator to reach a conclusion. Some attempts at conciliation, albeit in relation to substantial construction projects, have in fact led to this result, the effect of which is that the conciliation can continue for longer than a conventional arbitration. How the present rules work out in practice remains to be seen.

CONCLUSION

The procedure for disputes under the Minor Works Form is generally free of artificial restraints and pitfalls which may take a party by surprise. The keynote of the procedure is that the parties are required to make up their minds rapidly whether they wish to proceed from the Final Certificate to conciliation or arbitration. If Notice of Dispute is not served within 28 days, the Final Certificate becomes binding. The party serving the Notice to Refer then has a further 28 days to give notice either requiring conciliation or arbitration. If conciliation is adopted, then there is a further 28 day period after receipt of the conciliator's recommendations during which Notice to Refer to arbitration may be given in default of which, the recommendations become binding. If conciliation is adopted, it must normally be completed within 2 months, and a similar period is prescribed for arbitration under the ICE Procedure, Part F. Thus, unless the parties agree to change the rules, the process of dispute resolution should be rapid indeed and each party can look forward to the final determination of its rights and liabilities within these time periods. There is no good reason why these procedures should not be made to work. They should create a model of what construction arbitration can achieve.

TABLE OF CASES

Table of Cases